REMARKA

HOW TO GET OUT Oᵣ
YOUR OWN WAY AND
UNLEASH YOUR BRILLIANCE

DANIELLE MACLEOD

A NOTE ABOUT THE QUOTES IN THIS BOOK

All the quotes I've used here, have at some point featured on that great encyclopaedia of wisdom that is Facebook. I found them on Pinterest. I could have spent ages looking for something similar from really smart famous people and I chose not to.

Firstly, because this book is all about making things easy.

Secondly, because there are plenty of smart people out there who are not famous. You're probably one of them.

So I wanted to use them instead. Real people sending you real messages.

Whenever I could, I've cited the source. The exact source of some proved elusive to me. Whenever I couldn't find the author – regularly the case with quotes circulating the Internet, I've written, 'Unknown' rather than risk misattribution.

Enjoy.

Cover Design and Book Edit: Clarissa Design

The information contained within this book is strictly for educational purposes and is based on the author's personal thoughts.

The ideas are not intended to be a definitive set of instructions. If you wish to apply ideas contained in this book you are taking full responsibility for your actions.

First Edition: 2018

Published by Chaseville Press

Epub ISBN: 978-0-9935247-2-1

Version 1.0

TABLE OF CONTENTS

ABOUT THE AUTHOR

In 2016, Danielle Macleod decided to leave the corporate world and set up an organisation called Somebody Inside with Nic Devlin. Having started out in life wanting to be Prime Minister or maybe a librarian, she could never have envisaged becoming a leader of over 10,000 people in one of the UK's biggest blue chip corporates. More importantly, she could never have imagined that one day she would find a new way of being alive in the world. A way that enabled her to live with joy and from the heart. Giving up her corporate career to share those tools and techniques with other women turned out to be an easy decision and one that makes her smile every day.

Danielle lives in Edinburgh with her husband, John and Scruffy, their 16 year old rescue dog. Life has turned out to be Remarkably Easy after all.

INTRODUCTION

A BOOK FOR WOMEN?

I'm often asked, 'Why Women, Danielle? Men have these challenges too'. Yes, they do.

Sometimes I think that people initially have me pegged as an Angry Feminist. Or that deep down I don't like men very much. Or that I think women should rule the world. Let's clear that up now.

About five years ago, I happened to work for an organisation who asked me to be their 'poster girl' for their new Women in Leadership campaign. Literally. Giant posters. Some on toilet doors that I had to look at while having a wee. And YouTube videos filmed by TV pros that took hours to complete. It was an interesting time, especially because I couldn't see what all the fuss was about.

The thing about me is if I'm going to do something, I go all in. I wasn't up for being people's toilet read if I didn't believe in the message. After all, I had done brilliantly well in my career. At this point, I was leading 10,000 people. No-one could say being a woman had held me back. At least not right now. My time in construction many years earlier was a different story...

I got curious. I started with Sheryl Sandberg's book, 'Lean In' (who doesn't?) and went from there.

What I have come to realise more and more is that we live in a world that is defined by the male viewpoint. Don't believe me? Go into any bookstore right now and count how many white men have written books in the Top 20 non-fiction section. It's consistently more than 80%. As you know, white men are not 80% of the population of the world. Once you start looking, you'll notice it everywhere.

Whilst there are plenty of brilliant men out there doing amazing things (I'm very grateful to be married to an exceptional man), I believe the world right now is calling for balance and diversity. It's calling for the female voice in leadership as well as the male. And it's calling for representation from all races and all viewpoints.

I'm not an angry feminist on any level. I'm simply doing my part to bring balance to a world that is sorely in need of different perspectives and opinions and new ways of doing things. I truly believe that women are key to those changes.

This book is full of concepts that will work for men too. Indeed, men are welcome to read it and adopt any technique they find supportive and useful. It is intentionally written with women in mind. No compromise, a clear audience.

This book is about what I want for *you*. I want you out in the world shining bright, giving your light to those who need it. And it's for your tribe of women too. The ones who know what they really want and keep getting in their own way. The ones who get scared about whether they can do the things they dream of. The ones who believe they don't always deserve it.

It's time. And it could be oh so easy.

WHY READ THIS BOOK?

I've written this section about a gabillion times.

(Clearly, I'm exaggerating. That's not even a real number.)

Why? Because I want a different life for you than the one you have now. I want you to realise just what is possible if you get out of your own way.

- *I want you to realise that the only person standing IN your way is YOU.*

- *I want you to realise that the smallest changes can create the biggest transformations.*

- *I want you to realise that life gets easier the more you allow yourself to be you.*

That's why this book is all about you.

It's a book on how to listen to yourself more, and also less. It's a book about what happens when you step away from pleasing everyone else and start being who YOU are supposed to be.

It's also a book about the freedom that is waiting round the corner for you if only you would be willing to believe just what is possible when you make life easy and get out of the trap of believing everything has to be hard.

So why choose this book over all the others out there? *I know* what it's like to do and live through all the things I describe in here. *I know* you're too busy to make changes even though you want change. Most of all, *I know* the voice in your head that is the boss of you - the one that tells you you're not good enough and you should just play a wee bit smaller in case you get found out.

I also know that this book is really important. You see, I've learned over the years that people consistently believe that I have it nailed. They think they can't have what I have, because it's easier for me than it is for them. Yes, I'm a confident woman and yes, great things have happened in my life. That's far from the whole story. Factor in, two eating disorders, a business that almost made us bankrupt, a failed marriage, spinal surgery, family trauma that no-one would wish for. All those things too. So I want you to see that even I have this stuff going on. Because I know that when women look at me, they can't even imagine it. They couldn't even see it when I was in the very midst of those huge life lessons that I like to call a 'masterclass'.

I want you to know you are not alone.

I know what it's like to shift your relationship with that voice in your head, to lead your own life rather than allow the voice to lead yours.

I know what it's like to master fears and anxiety, and I know what it's like to drop back into them sometimes. And I also know what it's like to live with confidence, excitement and joy about what we can create and who we can be.

I want all of that for you.

In this book, I offer the tools for you to find your own path, rather than following mine.

We're going to have a good old laugh at ourselves too. We all do a lot of bonkers things that we hope no-one else notices. Well, I'm onto us. We're going to have fun.

ARE YOU READY TO MAKE A DIFFERENCE?

If you want a passive entertaining read, then this book might be OK and make you smile a few times.

If you want real change, more joy and excitement, and more of you living as your true self, then you're going to need to do it with me.

This is a book that requires reflection from you.

I've even created spaces in each chapter for you to do just that. So read it all the way through in one express go if you must (I'll be honest, I would), then come back and do it again with a pen or pencil and really think about what it means for you.

That second read will be the difference between insight and transformation vs information. Much of what I offer you in here, you already know (there's even a chapter on that specifically), my job is to offer it in a way that finally rings true for you.

Hear this though.

I've put the reflection pages in for a reason. Without them, you will skim through this book (some of you are going to do that anyway) and you won't create the change you long for. You might even blame the book. If you don't want to find a piece of paper, you could even write on the page. (Don't worry, you won't burn in hell). I'm making it easy for you. Make it easy on yourself. A skim read is not going to make the difference you're longing for.

The only way you will create the change you long for is if you *do the thinking* with attention and intention.

So if you have to read one chapter a week to make that happen, DO THAT.

It's time for the life *you* want to emerge.

WE'RE NOT THE SAME YOU AND I, AND YET WE ARE.

I know you think I'm not like you.

Sometimes I freak people out. I think big, I dream even bigger and I take action that often has others wide eyed.

Yet the same voices live inside my mind that are in yours. The voices of excitement and joy and the less appealing voices of fear and judgement. I used to hide mine well and they were always there. Some days they had me sobbing on the floor before heading off to my big six-figure job. Other days they would prevent me from leaving the house, even to be with my friends, because I didn't want people looking at me, talking about my fat body and how I had let myself go.

So the 'what' I choose to do in the world, and the 'how' and the scale of what I take on and the ways in which I attack myself are not the same as the choices that you make. They are unique to me. And yet, we are all wired to carry dreams and beliefs and love and fear. They are pretty much the same wherever you turn. That's what we have in common. It's those dreams and fears I am talking to as I write this.

It's the knowledge that when we commit our lives to the mastery of our own thoughts and give that attention before *anything* else, that we can change the game, exponentially. It's the realization that from this place, *everything* becomes easy.

You want the things *you* want in life. We have a tonne of things that make us different. We both have a mind that is equally as capable of creating amazing things and releasing magic in the world as it is of paralyzing us with fear and having us play small.

IS THIS BOOK REALLY FOR YOU?

Know this:

- *If you are a woman who has big dreams that are on a shelf right now, this is for you.*

- *If you're settling for 'one day' and 'some-day', this is for you.*

- *If you're sucking stuff up in the hope that it will be worth it in the long run and putting security before fulfilment this is for you.*

- *If things are going well, but you don't quite feel like you in the midst of it all, this is for you.*

- *If you're afraid that stepping up and creating what you really want is impossible or will cost you your financial wellbeing or your relationships or your safety, this is for you.*

I know all of these fears like they are my very best friends. I've been on the edge of bankruptcy, I've literally walked out of a dream job without even speaking to my boss or serving my notice. I've driven myself to depression and disordered eating on several occasions. I know the extremes and I also know the path out of them.

I'm offering you the shorter route. The easier route. The more playful route. I know how to create a life of joy and fulfilment and purpose. Right now, I'm offering you challenge, fun, expansion and shared experience.

There are questions in here that you need to think about the answers to. This is your time to dive into what you want and how to create it. Be it relationship, health, vocation, wealth, you name it. We're going to play with some great stuff!

For now hang onto these two things, because we'll be coming back to them a lot.

1. My life really changed when I DID THE LEAST and focused the most on THE THINGS I AM GOOD AT.

2. When I stopped listening to the voice in my head that perpetually told me to play small and hide my fat ugly body from the world, I started to realise that the only person who had ever held me back was me. And once you know that, well, you can start to live a whole lot differently.

In this book we're going to learn to fill our lives with less of the things that keep us busy and overwhelmed and much more of what we love, all the while, learning how to master that voice in our head that freaks the hell out of us.

That's the magic combination.

We carry so many ingrained beliefs about what is and isn't possible in our lives.

- All too often we believe that a life of impact means a life of sacrifice and taking the hard option. So we deny the impact we already have and we step away from what might be possible in order to protect what we already have.

- We all have this voice in our heads (you'll meet her shortly) that attacks viciously and berates us daily and we *never* talk about it to anyone. We seem to think we are the only one who experiences it. It keeps us small.

- We get tied up in obligation and duty, saying yes to everything and pleasing everyone and running around in busy, busy circles until we are too exhausted to remember who we are anymore.

I believe you are here on this planet for a reason.

Maybe you are bringing up a child who is going to be a revolutionary leader in the world. Maybe you are meant to change the patterns that have held generations of your family back for years. Maybe you are meant to be a beacon of love that changes others simply by showing up in your community with heart and generosity. Maybe you have a book or a song in you.

Maybe you have forgotten your dreams.

Maybe you are meant to change the world.

Ah, there it is. You see you *are* meant to change the world. All of those things are world changers. It's just you forgot for a minute.

You are meant to leave this world a little better than you found it.

It's time to create the life you really long for. Time to start owning your unique piece of brilliance in the world, whatever it might be. It's time to notice that the more you allow the wholeness of you out in the world, the easier it's all going to become.

That's where the magic is. We're waiting impatiently to be introduced to yours.

PRAISE FOR REMARKABLY EASY

REMARKABLY EASY IS A MUST READ FOR EVERY WOMAN.
IT'S THE QUINTESSENTIAL GUIDE FOR HOW TO STEP INTO
OUR AUTHENTICITY, OUR GENIUS, AND OUR POWER,
IN EVERY ASPECT OF LIFE. IT'S PURE ROCKET FUEL.

DANIELLE DELIVERS THIS EMPOWERING MESSAGE IN
HER UNIQUELY WITTY AND RELATABLE VOICE. SHE IS
A COMPASSIONATE ROLE MODEL AND A WHOLEHEARTED
CHAMPION OF WOMEN, ENCOURAGING EACH ONE OF US
TO OWN OUR POTENTIAL IN ORDER TO MAKE A BIGGER
IMPACT IN THIS WORLD. ILLUMINATING BRILLIANTLY WHERE
WE HAVE *CHOICE* AT EVERY TURN.

THE PROVOCATIVE QUESTIONS AT THE END OF EACH
CHAPTER MAKE HER INSIGHTS REMARKABLY ACTIONABLE
AS WELL. MY ADVICE? START CHOOSING "EASY" NOW:
BUY THIS BOOK, SCHEDULE A DATE WITH YOURSELF, AND
GET DEEPLY CURIOUS (IF NOT A LITTLE MESSY). PREPARE
FOR MASSIVE LIBERATION AND TRANSFORMATION!

SHELLEY PAXTON

LET THIS SINK IN

CHAPTER 1

ACCEPT THE LEADERSHIP ROLE IN YOUR LIFE

'YOU ARE FAR TOO SMART TO BE THE ONLY THING STANDING IN YOUR WAY.'

JENNIFER J FREEMAN

I know, I know, some of you are probably already thinking:

"Er, what? I didn't pick this up because of some big corporate job prospect. I picked it up because I wanted to change my life. That's what you said it was about!".

Breathe.

We still need to talk about leadership.

What if we looked at leadership as though it was the skill of simply and authentically *leading your own life to the very best of your capability?*

Well, then it gets interesting doesn't it?

If we see ourselves as leaders of *ourselves*, we might just start thinking a little differently.

If I was an exceptional leader of *me*, I would be creating what I wanted in the world:

- I would have intimate connection and relationships with the people in my life.

- I would inspire people to believe in me and support me in what I am doing, just by being me.

- I would be first in class at leading and modelling a way of living that I truly believe in.

- I would be an expert in making decisions about what is good for me and what is not.

- I would be doing the things that would transform my life.

Can you feel how incredible that would be?

Who doesn't want *that* kind of life?

That's the kind of leadership I'm taking about.

So when you shy away from the word 'leader' and say, *'Oh no, I'm not sure if that's truly me'*, you step back from what is possible for you. You miss out on practising the ideas and techniques that you could use to create what *you* want in the world.

As you keep reading all of the pages in this book, read them from this angle of leadership. The one where you are the very best leader of you that you can be.

Look at yourself in the mirror as if you were a leader every single day.

In fact, from this point forward, regard yourself as a queen. A woman who has a role to fulfil in the world whether she likes it or not or believes she is good enough or not.

Wake up every morning and ask yourself this:

'How can I be the very best leader of me in my life?'

Frankly, if you don't lead you well, who is going to? Do you want someone else to do it for you? *Really?*

Pause for a minute. If you've really taken that in I'm aware there's a strong chance that you're already wondering whether this is a bit self-centred and selfish.

That's another way the voice in your head holds you back.

There's enough space for *all* of us.

Besides, I have a strong hunch (backed up by a fair amount of personal evidence) that asking yourself this very question and leading from it can bring about mind blowingly incredible things for other people as well as you.

Just think about it.

Starting your life each day by asking this question and taking action on the answer means that:

- You show up in the world truly authentically, which means no-one has to spend any time working out your motives.

- The people in your relationships get to understand exactly what you want and have real clarity on your boundaries.

- You never spend any time holding yourself back or playing down your talents, which means *everyone else* gets to benefit from them.

- You inspire others around you by showing just *how* to live life to its fullest.

Check out that last bullet point again.

Sometimes you forget that people learn more from what they *see* than what they are *told*. In fact, I would go further and say that very often people rebel against what they are told. They ignore it almost entirely.

This is so important to get your head around. Especially if you are a mother.

If you tell your children you want the very best for them in life and you want them to live their dreams, and then you consistently model, day in and day out, sacrificing your dreams for others, what is it you think they learn?

Ah, now you're thinking.

They learn how to sacrifice their dreams for others whilst carrying a deep desire that others will fulfil their dreams as a consequence. Then when they have children, they teach them the exact same thing.

There's a smart legacy. Not quite what you meant to put out there, right?

Didn't think so.

It's time to step into a new way of being, where you commit to being the very best leader of your life that you can be.

YOU ALREADY KNOW HOW TO PLAY SMALL. NOW IT'S TIME TO PLAY BIG

You know that place where the inner voice of fear stabs at your heart? You're familiar with knowing something to be true and yet being wholly unable to move on from it. You may be aware that your unwillingness to every step into your brilliance leads to nothing but self- abuse and tightness in your mind and often in your relationships and yet for some reason, some part of you wants to *hold onto it for dear life*.

You also know what it feels like to have one or more parts of you that you obsess with being able to change every single day – be it your confidence, your body, your voice, your brain.

Now you need to know just how much those obsessions and fears hold you back.

Can we take them away forever?

I believe there are people who have mastered the art of living in this way in such a way that you would feel it simply standing next to them. These people have dedicated their life to it as a singular mission. They live their lives in contemplation, self- awareness and untouchable peace. It's incredible to be in their presence.

Am I one of them? No. I choose to lead a life of contemplation *combined* with momentum and impact. I want to be in action. So I choose to be out in the world trying out new ideas and loving the joy of *doing* as well as *being*. I choose to question and challenge what is going on around me and I choose to fuel my anger and passion for injustice into making change. I'm not looking for that level of mastery. At least not right now. I've learned to love this about myself.

As a consequence of studying with and from some of these people who have found inner peace at the greatest level as well as many other exceptional teachers in the world, what has changed for me is I can make those negative inner voices so much smaller. I know how to lessen their impact. I know ways to stop one bad day becoming 10 or 15 or 20 or even 6 months. I want that for you.

I have a life where I can accept bad moments and move on from them. Life twists and turns. It throws us curve balls all the time. I have stopped stretching them out, stopped breathing more life into them.

In fact, if I'm honest, I can't think of the last time I even labelled something as 'bad'. There might have been moments I wouldn't have chosen to experience given the opportunity, and I don't let them fill my mind with guilt or shame or anger. They are in the past. Moments that can never be altered or changed. How does it serve me to still live in them as if they are occurring now? Why would I let them have so much power?

THE BEST LEADERS OF THEMSELVES ENDED THEIR WAR WITH THEMSELVES LONG AGO

The best leaders have learned to embrace themselves for who they are. They have accepted their flaws and imperfections, even if they don't always love them and in doing so, have opened up more space in their minds and lives than you can even imagine.

They realised that the suffering in their lives was self-inflicted; that they had been twisting a knife in their hearts without even realising it. As soon as they realised it, they got on with the business of learning how to stop.

The lightbulb moment you are looking for that you haven't yet seen is this:

it IS all about you after all.

You have the power to change it all, and as the Wizard of Oz quote goes, *'You had the power all along'*.

It's time to uncover the space in your mind that allows you to get on and be who you want to be in the world. That space that enables you to embrace clarity and step beyond fear, the space that gives you permission to practice new things with excitement instead of self-admonishment and shrinking.

It is that space that allows you to expand and live freely as the very best leader of you.

Just imagine... Hours of your day where the voice in your head is not giving you grief for what you have not done. All that precious time to be alive and in love with life. All that capability to breathe in and notice what is actually happening around you in this very moment.

Just imagine what you can create from there.

Got it? Great. Reflect some more on the next page before we say hello to the one who creates all the trouble

REFLECTION

1. *How can I be the best leader of my own life? What does that even mean to me?*

2. *What would it feel like to own my brilliance in the world?*

3. *What would I be doing with my life if I wasn't afraid or self attacking?*

CHAPTER 2

INTRODUCING YOUR CRAZY LADY

'I HAVE TO REMIND MYSELF ALL THE TIME THAT BEING
AFRAID OF THINGS GOING WRONG ISN'T THE WAY TO
MAKE THEM GO RIGHT.'

UNKNOWN

Let's get her onstage first.

She'll like that.

She craves attention this one. Except then she kind of
doesn't. In fact she's a bit of a paradox really. Confused little
soul when you get to know her. You know who I mean, right?
Your very own Crazy Lady - that voice inside you that says:

'You're not as good as you think you are.'

*'I TOLD YOU, you couldn't do it, and you had to go try
anyway didn't you?'*

'No-one likes a show off.'

'HOW are we ever going to survive now?!'

*'DON'T DO IT. IT'S DANGEROUS AND YOU'RE NOT
GOOD ENOUGH!'*

*'Don't speak right now. People in here know more than you.
You'll make a fool of yourself.'*

'You're just an embarrassment to the world.'

It's quite some repertoire she has going. On and on and on.
You know it, I know you do.

The difference between you and me is you *feel* this as OUCH.
PAIN. I just hear, 'Blah, blah, blah'...

9

Here's a little secret I'm not sure you're in on yet.

Everyone has one. *Everyone.* She's our hidden shame. We don't like to admit she exists, even though she hangs around with us a lot of the time. All of the time pretty much. We kind of hope that if we ignore her and pretend she's not there she'll go away.

Hardly any of us ever mention her. Which is odd really, because essentially every time a bunch of women get together, you can guarantee that at least some of us have brought our Crazy Lady along too. (She's the one telling you to suck in your stomach or avoid the cake, or wait to see if everyone else is having a drink before you have one, in case you look like you're on the verge of alcoholism...).

Funnily enough, when we learn to talk about her, we diminish her power. Almost immediately.

We really should have more of those conversations.

Your Crazy Lady is fear. She senses danger and she steps into full-on reptile response. Fight, Flight or Freeze. The thing is, her instincts are generally a bit off.

Actually, let's be clear. Her instincts are *dreadful*. She predicts the future with very little accuracy indeed, although she probably makes more noise than almost anyone you know. Here are some examples of how bad her instincts are:

- If you speak up in a meeting, on the whole, the risk of ruining the rest of your ENTIRE life or being killed on the spot is pretty slim.

- If you eat that cake, the risk of you eating yourself to death, well, it doesn't go up all that much to be honest.

- If you acknowledge a nice thing about yourself, it's not that likely that tomorrow you will be front page of the world's newspapers crowned, 'Most Arrogant Woman of the Year'.

YOU DON'T NEED TO GIVE HER QUITE AS MUCH SPACE AS YOU DO.

'Ah, but I don't give her any space at all, Danielle. I shout at her and tell her to shut the hell up'.

Yep. You might want to rethink that approach. Working for you so far?

The thing about that method is you're *trying to kill off a part of you*. Whatever way you look at that approach, it's not going to work. It's like trying to persuade ourselves that eating food is bad – we *need* food to survive (spotted that one yet, serial dieters out there?). The brain simply can't handle these kinds of contradictions.

You can't kill her off without killing yourself. *You can't hurt her without hurting you.*

Starting a battle with yourself, it's not a smart thing lady. From today we stop it.

We change the relationship.

Think of it like a rope tied around your wrist. It has one of those clever knots on it that the Scouts talk about (I'd love to give you the name, it's just I never listened in those sessions). You know what I mean though, if you resist, it tightens more.

That's what it's like with your Crazy Lady. When you resist her, she constricts. *You* constrict. It all gets that little bit harder.

What you are looking for is *expansion*. Which requires a gentler approach. It requires a little lightening up and letting go.

For those of you ready to hear this, if I'm honest, it requires surrender, which is probably bringing you out in hives at the very thought.

For now though, and whenever Crazy Lady pops in with her opinions as you take steps forward, you just need to smile, say, *'I love you, you bonkers old thing, and I've heard ALL of this before. So you'll have to excuse me while I just get on with it. You do the fear thing. I choose love'*.

It's not as simple as that of course, but start here.

Choose love. Of yourself first and then others. Simples.

REFLECTION

1. *When did I last hear from my Crazy Lady?*

2. *In this moment, now I'm really listening out for her, how often is she really around?*

3. *If I really tune into what she's saying, what is she most afraid of?*

4. *What do I think could happen if I simply started to love myself more? (Include fears and good things).*

CHAPTER 3

THE STUFF YOU ALREADY KNOW

'I NEVER MAKE THE SAME MISTAKE TWICE. I MAKE IT LIKE FIVE OR SIX TIMES, YOU KNOW, JUST TO BE SURE.'

UNKNOWN

I'm going to be really honest with you right now. There's very little, if anything at all that I am going to say in this book that you do not know already. Sometimes, I am going to be stating the bleeding obvious. And I am still going to do it.

Do you know why?

Because so many women do this thing, where they nod and smile and say, *'I know,'* and then they crack on doing the same old bonkers stuff they were doing before.

So many women pretend to themselves that they are going to make a change and find themselves hooked on their old way of doing things, afraid of letting go, believing their way will work for them if only they could be harder on themselves, improve certain things, keep on keeping on.

So many women sign up to online programmes and don't do them, start diets or exercise programmes, or decide to give up whatever vice they think needs to be gone from their lives, commit to leaving work earlier, checking the iPhone less...

You name it, we're always deciding we're going to change something.

So many women do so many of these things.

I believe we miss two important points every time we decide we are going to make a change:

- **We blatantly lie to ourselves**

Now, now, don't be offended. We do. All the time.

You start a diet when you desperately want to lose weight, *even though deep down you have no desire whatsoever to put yourself through another diet regime.*

You promise to yourself and those around you that you are going to leave work early at least two nights a week to be home with your partner or your kids, *even though deep down you have not worked through your core belief that everything will go to hell if you don't remain in the office every time a minor crisis emerges at 5pm.*

You declare loud and proud that you will go for a run twice a week, *even though you can practically already feel the comfort of the sofa and the tub of ice cream that is calling your name softly from the freezer. And you're oh, so tired right now...*

You already know you are not going to do it.

So, from today, it's time to start EXAMINING YOUR TRUTH before embarking on another change that is predestined to failure (thus proving to your Crazy Lady, once again, that you never actually complete anything you have started).

When you examine your truth, you can make entirely different decisions.

LIGHT BULB MOMENT

Let me give you a recent example of a supermarket trip with my husband.

As we worked our way along the aisles, he leaned over to pick up a packet of sun-blush tomatoes (who knows what these things are really for?). As he leaned over to put them in the trolley, I said, 'Honey, we definitely don't need those, we threw the last two packets away'.

(I *hate* throwing food away).

He looked at me, and said, 'I know, but I'll definitely eat these ones, I really need to get into the habit of eating better. I'm eating crap at the moment'.

Because he knows all about examining truths, (he's lived with me a long time), I looked him square in the eye and said,

'I absolutely understand that. If you really listen to what your intentions are, are you just *wanting to change,* or are you *going to make a change*? Because we can buy them if you're going to do it and let's not waste them if you're hoping you might manage to persuade yourself'.

He looked right at me, smiled, and put those tomatoes back on the shelf.

'I'm not ready. They won't get eaten'.

BOOM.

Do you see the permission in there?

Do you see the liberation in dropping the 'I should be doing something different' and simply accepting that deep down, now is not the time?

Once we get curious about what we are saying and the commitments we are making we can make different choices:

- We can choose to accept that right now we are simply not going anywhere near that change.

- We can choose a gentler path with a softer progression.

- We can find alternatives that may meet the same need and in ways we find more appealing or manageable.

- We can choose to seek out sources of motivation that will help us get out of our inaction into what we want to create.

- We can choose to examine what is going on at a deeper level and assess what we really need to do next.

We can remove so much of the inner battle that we put ourselves through when we try to persuade ourselves that we are going to make a change that we already know we are not going to do. We can notice that our mind is frantically trying to hold two entirely different positions (the mind is so clever!) and we can just breathe through it and accept where we are right now.

We can save ourselves a lot of heartache. On some occasions, also a fair bit of money. Which is always a bonus.

Speak your truth to you, for goodness sake. *You know it already.*

- **We attack ourselves violently when we smell a failure**

This one is brutal.

We create this wonderful scenario when we take on change that we know deep down we have no intention of doing.

We start things that we are pretty much predestined to fail at.

The diet commences on Monday morning, only to be blown by Monday evening (because we've eaten an apple and a few crackers all day and so *of course* we are starving when we get home, this isn't willpower, it's *biology*).

Since we've failed so spectacularly, Crazy Lady gets to bring out all her big guns.

She gets to remind us that we *never finish anything that we start.*

She gets to show us that we are a *total and complete failure.*

She sobs violently that we are probably going to *eat ourselves to death.*

Somehow that highly useful advice ends in both of us gorging on pizza and chocolate and whatever else is in the house without tasting any of it because now she's shouting, 'NOOOOO. THIS IS BAD. STOOOOOOP!'

And since it is The Law that you can only start diets on Mondays, we now have permission to eat all the food in the house (and probably go out and buy some more on Sunday night to make sure we get all the good stuff in) so that we can, er, not start the diet again next week.

Sigh.

Exhausting, hurtful and self-destructive.

Imagine if your mum and dad had taught you to walk that way?

Imagine if your very first attempt at a step, where you inevitably fell over, was followed with,

'Good grief child, are you stupid? Can't you do anything we ask you to? How hard can it be? One step that's all we're asking of you, and you can't even manage that'.

And after an hour or so of that conversation, they'd put you back in your bed until next Monday when you were allowed to have another go under scrupulous supervision.

You'd have grown up a very different person.

Remember this chapter is all about the stuff you already know.

You already know the road of self-attack ends up in quite the opposite destination to Joy.

You already know that telling yourself you've failed and are a total failure in life is probably the worst technique imaginable for getting you back on your feet again (unless you're in one of those really dramatic movies when that spit on your face as you lie in the dirt is the very last straw. And who wants to create that scenario in their life?).

You already know the analogy about the child walking.

I am not telling you anything new.

Instead of that being a bad thing, *look at it properly.*

Go on, really - Take. It. In.

You know this stuff and yet for the whole of your life you remain *totally committed to your path of completely ignoring it.*

For some reason your mind has you believing that just one more attempt at this method that has so far, *never worked for you,* just one more attempt, and you will have it nailed.

I'll tell you what, if you're really sure, shall we bet a month's salary on it?

Hmm, didn't think so.

FORGIVE AND RECOMMIT.

As luck would have it, I have a new technique. My business partner, Nic, taught it to me and let me tell you, it is one of my mantras for life. Three words: Forgive and Recommit. It's that simple.

Let's break that down so it really sinks in. Because there's a chance that on this occasion you have decided to listen to what you already know. There's a chance a little voice in you has whispered, *'Er, I think she's onto something here'* and that you have decided it's time to try something different. (PS that little voice is not the Crazy One, you can listen this time).

We want to capitalise on that fast.

Let's go back to the diet analogy again.

You've come home, having half-starved yourself all day. No surprise, you're agitated because you are *hungry* and also somewhat void of energy. Because you're tired and hungry, you've probably been thinking about what's in the fridge all the way home (even though you've been pretending you don't know that the fridge is *exactly* where you're going when you finally get through the doors. In fact, you'll probably barely put your bag down).

You open the fridge and there it is. Thank goodness. The thing you have been imagining. (For me, it's cheese, so we'll go with cheese for now. I'm already salivating...).

There it is, all pretty and happy in its wrapping, just waiting for you to eat a tiny bit so that you can make your dinner without the ravenous dog in your belly yapping it's head off.

You take a knife and the cheese to the kitchen counter and cut a piece off and somewhere in the midst of time and space, it disappears in the blink of an eye like a magic trick.

You have no recollection whatsoever of eating it and your stomach is hardly saying *'oh, thank you for the lovely food. Now I feel great!'*.

This naturally means you'd better cut off another bit. Then another and another and another and every time you do it, Crazy Lady is like, *'ARE YOU KIDDING ME? You're having MORE? You know how bad this stuff is for you, right?'* and she is getting more and more panicked, meaning you need to dissipate the noise even more.

The best strategy we know for this is, um... Eat more cheese.

Throughout this whole interaction between you, Crazy Lady and the third party cheese, you have options.

You can give the reins over to Crazy Lady or you can develop a practice of noticing, which warms me up nicely into forgiveness.

'Oh look, here I am eating the cheese. That's interesting. No wonder really, I'm pretty hungry. Well, let's put this in perspective, I'm not committing mass murder here, I'm eating a bit of cheese'.

Yes, in many ways it's a blip on the plan and equally, you can forgive yourself for a bit of cheese.

'Thanks for the danger signs Crazy Lady, useful warning, and don't you be worrying. I'm just having a bit of cheese and then I'm going to make that lovely <insert whatever it is you were planning to have as a nutritious nourishing meal for dinner> and we can sit and enjoy it together. I'm still committed to this. It's just that today I'm going to have a little bit more than I planned'.

Ta Daaaah...! Forgive and recommit.

Here's the really great news:

you can do this at any stage in the process - even if you have eaten every bit of food in the house.

You can say to yourself, *'Gosh, I really would have preferred to have chosen something different - And I didn't - And the world is still turning and I am still committed to caring for myself. It's OK. I am doing the best I can and even though it's not the best I would have liked, it is what it is'.*

And then go again.

Rinse and repeat.

Every single time.

The moment you step into self-compassion, Crazy Lady tones down a little. She likes to be heard. She likes to know her voice counts. You're acknowledging she has a point, you're reassuring her you're still in it and you're making it clear there's no real danger.

Forgive. Recommit.

It's that simple.

You gain *nothing* from constantly attacking yourself from failure except a bunch of internal bruises.

NOTHING.

You wouldn't advise anyone to get a stick out and keep bashing themselves till they finally did the thing they said they were going to do, so don't apply that technique to yourself expecting it to work.

This system you have been applying for pretty much all of your life is rubbish. You don't need to try harder, you need to love and accept yourself more.

You know that already by the way. Here I am, just reminding you again.

#sorrynotsorry.

REFLECTION

1. *What am I pretending I am going to start in the near future that deep down I have no intention of doing?*

2. *What would happen if I just let it go for a while? What's my fear if I don't?*

3. *Where can I introduce the practice of Forgive and Recommit to my life?*

CHAPTER 4

THE THINGS YOU TELL YOURSELF ABOUT TIME

'INSTEAD OF SAYING, "I DON'T HAVE TIME", TRY SAYING, 'IT'S NOT A PRIORITY' AND SEE HOW THAT FEELS.'

UNKNOWN

This is the top 'getting out of doing something' response I hear. By a very long margin.

'I just don't have enough time' <sigh>.

Excuse me while I just go bang my head against a wall for a minute.

You don't have time to create the life you long for?

Keep reading that sentence over and over and over again till it sinks in.

You haven't read it enough. Honestly, go again.

Have you got it yet?

What on earth are you spending your time on if it's not on the *things you really want?*

YOU'VE ONLY GOT ONE LIFE

You remember I said before that we often know something to be true, and yet we seem unwilling to integrate it into our lives?

Here's another one for you:

you've only got one life.

Watch your mind with this one. Watch it right now. Because it's either nodding vigorously and saying, *'yes, OF COURSE I know that'* or it's sighing and saying, *'yes, I know that, but you just don't understand...'*.

Either way, have you actually got this into your head yet?

You have only got ONE life. ONE opportunity to live full out as this glorious unique version of you in the world who will never exist again in time and space. ONE.

So what are you doing letting all that precious time pass by on a bunch of things that don't help you create and grow and nurture the things you love? What are you doing not devoting every breath you have to creating more love, more passion, more joy, more impact in your life?

CAN'T, SHOULD, MUST...

You know what it is, don't you?

You've got all caught up in, *'got to'*, and *'can't'*, *'should'* and *'must'*.

I love all the words in the world. Well, nearly all of them. There's a couple of profanities that you won't find coming out of my mouth because they're a step too far.

'Can't' and 'should' and 'must' not so much.

This is a challenge, because I like to love everything. So if I was going to fall in love with those words, this is why:

they show us when we are lying to ourselves, which makes them very useful words indeed.

You see, there is no such thing as 'got to' or 'must'. You always have a *choice*. You might not like the choice you have, and you *always* have one.

Let me give you the most extreme example I can think of.

Marshall Rosenberg, the creator of the world renowned Nonviolent Communication Methodology and author of many books on the subject, describes a time when he was explaining this very concept to a group of people who were living in a nation experiencing dangerous times. I'm paraphrasing and here's the essence of the story:

A man in the group looked at him indignantly and said, *'How can you say that's true? We do not always have a choice. Recently, I was dragged out of my car and held at gunpoint. The weapon-holder told me to strip my clothes or he would kill me.'*

'So you had a choice,' Marshall replied, *'Strip or die. What did you choose?'*

Realising what he had said, the man smiled, *'Ah. I kept my clothes on. Even though I was not sure what would happen, I made a decision. And I am still here. I had a choice. Whatever I chose, I had a choice'.*

It wasn't a 'fun' choice, it was still a choice. There is *always* choice. In almost every scenario, there are *infinitely* more choices than you allow yourself. For some reason we love to only play with two, which in itself is limiting. Stay with this though.

When you say you have no time (especially when you really mean, no choice), check in.

Is it true?

Is it *really* true?

Because I'm willing to bet there are days you do this thing I like to call numbing. Where you so dislike the space around you that you scroll social media for hours and hours. Where you stick on the television and then don't even watch it because you've got the Book of Face on the go anyway. Where you sit with a bottle of wine and drink to relax because you can't handle your frustration anymore. Where you go shopping to get food because you can't be bothered with the food in the cupboard and before you know it, you've lost an hour and a half just by popping into the supermarket, wandering round and getting home again.

Or you're doing that other thing where you do what you think everyone else wants you to do so that you don't offend or upset the applecart or ruin the image of you as great friend, great daughter, great mother, great wife, great boss. That thing where you agree to run around like a mad person sorting out other people's stuff when every bone in your body is crying for rest. That thing where you end up in this crazy trading war that never quite works out in your favour, figuring that if you do stuff for other people they'll do stuff back from you and then resenting them when they turn out to have their own boundaries pretty well defined.

You might even be one of those amazing mothers who is bringing up children telling them they can be anything they want to in the world, whilst beautifully modelling to them how to live a life of total self-sacrifice and wondering why they choose the same.

Whatever you're doing, you have got time. You've got the same amount of time as the rest of us.

How you choose to spend it is up to you.

If you were willing to dedicate even 20 minutes a week to crafting and creating the life you long for and learning how to become a leader of you in your life, do you realise that's 0.002% of the time you have available to you in any week?

You can't spare 0.002% of your time to focus on CREATING THE LIFE YOU LONG FOR?

You couldn't play that podcast in the car *on the way* to the supermarket?

You couldn't read that book *while* you were drinking the glass of wine?

Let's get really clear, this is *always* about choices.

And if you're resenting how your time is being spent right now, there's a good chance it has a lot to do with the stories you hold in your head about who you should be and how you must behave.

Underneath all of that, it almost certainly has to do with how much you believe that being all you can be is going to turn out just brilliantly. It has to do with fear again.

So right now, I'm just going to believe for you.

All you have to do is keep reading and answering the questions. I've got you covered.

In the meantime, let's not be blaming time any more. That's just a diversion tactic. It's bullshit.

The sooner you get your head around the fact that you are creating your own life, exactly the way it is, the sooner you can own your decisions, and the sooner all the power to create is back in your hands.

Exactly where it should be.

REFLECTION

1. Where are all the spaces in my life that I find myself saying 'I must', 'I have to', 'I should'?

2. Re-write them all to say, 'I choose to...'.

3. How do I feel now? Do I want to change my mind about any of them as a consequence? What changes am I going to make, if any?

Your choice. ALWAYS your choice.

THE FOUR PRACTICES THAT WILL OPEN UP YOUR WORLD

CHAPTER 5

HARD VS EASY

'WHETHER YOU THINK YOU CAN, OR THINK YOU CAN'T.
YOU'RE RIGHT.'

HENRY FORD

Here's where it gets fun, although it's possible you're already thinking:

'Bet it's not as easy as she says it is. She's probably got a tonne of money and she for sure doesn't live the life I do'.

Of course I don't. Even so, maybe it is a whole lot easier than you think. Once you get out of your own way...

It would be difficult to number how many women I have coached or been in conversation with, who refuse to own any of their talents in life. These women believe they are 'lucky' and rarely credit themselves with the things they have achieved. They pull a face when you point out to them that it's almost impossible that they didn't have something to do with the thing that they created so beautifully.

LIGHT BULB
MOMENT

I used to do this too.

I remember having a conversation with my incredible Coach at the time, Elaine, about how it 'didn't count' that I had spearheaded a fundraising campaign that ended up bringing in over £120,000 to build a school in India (this was even more amazing because we had only committed £50,000).

She gave me a look, 'It doesn't count?'

'No.' I said, 'In the end it turned out to be easy.'

'Ah' she said. Accompanied by another one of those looks.

'So it only counts if it's hard?'

'Well, yes' I replied, keen to point out my lack of contribution, 'you know when I set out to do this, I had no idea if it was even possible, but what happened was as I started to ask for help, a gang of amazing people stepped up and they did so much! I found that if I just leaned into my network and my job title in the organisation, I could get hold of all kinds of things I never knew I could and that people would respond when I asked them to buy tickets or get involved. So it wasn't me who made it happen you see? It was other people'.

She did well not to put her head in her hands at this point.

'Danielle,' (now I know I'm getting an important message), 'YOU rang the charity and committed the money, YOU asked for volunteers, YOU put your name against it and asked people to help, donate, send things, do whatever they could. And they responded. If you had not started this, it would never have happened'.

I squirmed. She continued.

'Why does everything have to be hard in your life for it to count? What if all you did was things you found easy? How many more schools would there be then? Because surely what REALLY counts, is that those children HAVE A SCHOOL to go to?'.

And there it was. My first real look at yet another story I had carried all of my life.

The story of, 'If it's easy, I must have struck it lucky'. Which meant I definitely couldn't celebrate it.

It only counted if it felt truly hard.

It only counted if I had to pour blood sweat and tears into it.

It only counted if it hurt a bit.

Otherwise, I had simply been in the right place at the right time. Anyone could have done it.

This story shows up so many times, it's like a disease amongst women! That when good things happen and it didn't hurt to get them, well, luck just happened to be on our side. We had nothing to do with it. This then perpetuates the belief that to create impact, to create what we want in the world, it has to be *hard*.

Let's drop that right now. Because a life of flow and ease is a secret longing for many of us:

- What if you could have it *at work* as well as in your relaxation time?

- What if you trusted your talents so much that you simply focused on using them more and more?

- What if, as a consequence of doing that, things became easier and easier?

- What if you started to own your own unique flavour of brilliance?

- What if, in believing a little more in yourself, you not only discovered easy, but also realised that it is a wonderful experience to have?

- What if everything didn't have to come the hard way?

You don't believe me do you?

Sigh. I get it.

For a while I wouldn't have believed me either.

So, try this as a daily practice.

It's called,

'What if there was an easier way?'

You get to put this into practice every single time life feels too hard or you are frustrated with the choices you believe you have to make.

You just ask yourself the question,

'How can I make this easy?'

My business partner Nic and I do this all the time. *'How can I make this easy?'* has become our North Star. Every time something in our business or life feels hard, we ask the question.

Because what you start to see after a while is that often you are making it hard for yourself. Sometimes out of a sense of perfectionism, sometimes because you haven't even checked in with the stories you tell yourself.

LIGHT BULB
MOMENT

Here's a really simple example.

Nic and I were together having a bit of a chat before we got down to work (we are exceptionally good at chatting). A friend of ours had a birthday coming up and she had asked for money or vouchers.

Nic gets out her Present Box (yes, she has a Present Box) and checks out her vouchers (I know, I was blown away too, the Present Box even has gift vouchers in it). She has £35 of vouchers for our favourite department store. This is not good enough however, because she wants to give our friend £40 since it's her 40th birthday.

Within two minutes, she has created a plan to change her already super busy day to get the bus into town, go to said department store, get £5 more of vouchers and come home.

The thought of it is stressing her out, but she's already resigned to sucking it up.

Except she has a whole tonne of cash sitting next to the vouchers.

In service of making it easy, I suggest she give our friend cash.

Nic is horrified, 'Cash? I can't give her cash!'.

Honestly, you would think I had suggested she decorate the birthday card with bogeys.

It turns out she has a long held belief that cash is the indication of a bad inconsiderate friend (notwithstanding the fact that she has already handcrafted a card for her). As a consequence, the fact that our friend has actually *asked for cash* has completely passed her by, it has been dismissed. It doesn't fit with her belief that cash for birthdays is a bad thing.

FACEPALM.

Of course the ending to the story is, she sees sense, our friend gets exactly what she wanted for her birthday anyway, and Nic has two hours back in her day.

EVERYONE WINS.

Your mission is to make things easier in your life.

That way you will have time to do more stuff. You will enjoy more of what you do and before you even get to the destination you are now gliding towards with grace and ease, you already have grace and ease.

Who would have thought it?

I've got this feeling you're nodding your head a lot right now (this is another one of those things you know you know), so you know what, here's a BONUS STORY, and one that is work related in case the home stories don't cut it for you.

LIGHT BULB MOMENT

When we kicked off our business, Somebody Inside, Nic and I had a conversation about how we wanted to create opportunities for women to spend time with us to expand their impact and to get into deep connection and conversation.

Yes, we wanted to create a network.

Oh good grief, NO WE DID NOT. Because we think networking events are one of those excruciatingly painful things that someone somewhere along the line told us were important to building our career.

So we wanted to build a network that was *not* a network.

I agreed with Nic that I would draft up some ideas so that we could talk about them the next time we got together. (I like doing idea drafting, this is fun for me).

Except as I started to write, I realised I was completely stuck on what on Earth to call it. How could I draw women to what could easily be described as a networking event when we wanted them to believe it would be nothing like networking?

I spent quite some time trying to come up with a smart name. (You may be familiar with the waking in the night moments of genius that are totally rubbish in the light of day). It was going to need to be *really smart*. So women would get it and love it. I was convinced it was all in the name.

I realised I was overthinking it. So I left it to simmer in my subconscious, trusting it would have a great idea (another favourite technique). Nothing. Nada. I am all out of smarts.

And then I realise. This could hold us back for a long, long time.

I realise, I am *making this hard*. Since my motto is make it easy, I give it absolutely no more thought whatsoever and I turned on the laptop to write this:

1. We're going to set up a new Women's Thing in Edinburgh. We're calling it a Thing, because Lord knows it is not going to be called a NETWORK and we haven't got a better name for it, so it's just going to be a Thing for now.

(Frankly, the fact that we're willing to call it a Thing and get it going anyway, should tell you, loud and clear that we are up for something different.)

2. Secondly, once it gets started, we cross our hearts promise that we will spend absolutely no time debating on whether it should be called anything other than a Thing. We will just get on with the actual purpose of it and love it for what it is. A Great Thing for Women.

See what I mean now? Even in work, with complicated problems – you can do this. You can *always* make it easier.

Oh, the relief. We have openly declared it will be called a Thing forever. Job done. Funnily enough, in the making it easy, we created exactly what we wanted anyway. Without the need to be all smart about it.

In fact, every time we write about it, turns out that calling it The Thing was actually a stroke of genius. It makes for amazing messages, like, *'This could be just The Thing you're looking for'*.

There's nothing we love more than hearing a woman turn to another woman and say, *'are you going to The Thing next month?'*.

Most importantly though, searching frustratedly for the spark of genius is not where the answer was. The answer came when I completely let it go and moved on.

So ask yourself the question,

'How can I make this easy?'

If you're not sure, ask it with someone else in the room. You may need their assistance for a while as you clear out some of those old beliefs that can be hard to spot when you've been living with them for a lifetime.

Just wait and see what happens.

It's one of the most fun practices I know.

Try it.

From this point onward, drop your ideas about hard lady, it does not serve you in any way.

Let's make it *EASY*.

REFLECTION

1. *What are the things in my life that feel hard right now?*

2. *Where do I find myself running out of time or creating jobs that take ages?*

3. *What would I need to do to make this stuff easy?*

CHAPTER 6

TURNING PRACTICE INTO PLAY

'WHAT SCREWS US UP MOST IN LIFE IS THE PICTURE IN
OUR HEAD OF HOW IT'S SUPPOSED TO BE.'

(THERE'S A LOT OF PEOPLE ON GOOGLE
CLAIMING SOCRATES WROTE THIS.

EXCUSE MY SCEPTICISM, IF YOU DID SOCRATES,
YOUR LANGUAGE WAS WELL AHEAD OF TIME)

On a logical level, I think we all get that practice is a requirement in life.

I think we get that we have to make mistakes in order to get better at something. I think many of us (especially those of us who lead people) run around saying, 'Oh yes, I totally believe in the power of mistakes and learning'.

That's fine as it goes, except, when we *need* to get it perfect.

And then practising, and making mistakes, well that's a pretty rubbish idea.

The thing is, we seem to need to get it perfect quite a lot of the time. In fact, it seems to me, we're only really willing to practise when we're totally relaxed about the outcome.

For example, it's unlikely, in my life, that I'm going to practise a brand new recipe when I have friends coming round for dinner. Unless they're my very closest friends indeed and I know we can have a laugh about anything, I'm probably not going to try and bake some complicated cake that has plenty of margin for error in it if there's any real chance that I might be presenting them with some kind of melting chocolate slop at the end of the evening. Remember Bridget Jones and the Blue Soup? Who wants to be *that* hostess?

This means, in all reality, I will probably never make that cake that looks totally yummy in my recipe book, because I'm not really up for buying all the ingredients and spending hours making it look perfect, so that me and my husband can have it after our sausage sandwich for dinner (it's all glamour in our house). That feels like an awful lot of effort for a practice run.

And if I do get round to making it, and it turns out to be pretty hard and it all goes a bit wrong, and my kitchen looks, well, like it does after my husband has been cooking at the end of it, there's very little chance then that I will make it again.

And that's just baking a cake...

(For some of you budding chefs in the making, I know that your cake could have been my equivalent of an executive presentation, you get my drift though, right? That's not even something where my reputation is on the line in any sense. And even then, er, no thanks.)

So, yep, I buy into practicing and making mistakes *in theory*.

In practice, if I'm really honest, I kind of like things to be perfect.

Me and almost every woman I know.

The best advice I ever got on this one, was from a lady called Julia Cameron, the author of the brilliant and timeless book, 'The Artist's Way'. Her book is one of several I have read on how to unleash our creativity. (You don't need to be an 'artist' to benefit from it.)

In the book, she refers to budding screenwriters. She points out that the problem is,

We all compare our PRACTICE to someone else's PERFECT.

In her example, young screenwriters are comparing their work to that of George Lucas.

She points out that they never compare their work to George Lucas' first film script (I'm guessing that it's probably not even available to read), they compare it to Star Wars, his world renowned piece of brilliance. They fall short and they stop. Because they have no idea how to write something as good as Star Wars.

Of course they don't.

Nor did George Lucas when he started.

They need to *practise.*

WE need to practise.

Keep with me on this one. I know you haven't got it yet, at the heart level.

You know when you were a kid and someone gave you a recorder to play... and you picked it up and you parped out some awful noise that your poor parents had to listen to for weeks on end? Well some of you, you got pretty good at it. You graduated onto other instruments.

A few of you, well you got so good at those other instruments, that you aced all your exams and you got to play in school concerts. Some of you even went to University to get even better. And even though you had been practising for years, you had to keep on practising. Some days, you totally hoofed it up. For your sake, I'm hoping that's not when you were playing solo on a big stage, but it might have been.

Some days, we will *all* totally hoof it up.

But if we start to *own* that we have talent and then we get excited about what could happen if we were only willing to practise dialing it up. Well, that becomes an adventure, doesn't it?

GETTING BETTER AT WHAT YOU'RE GOOD AT

When we get onto establishing what you are *already* good at, you need to commit to practising *getting even better*.

The good news is, you're already good at it, so it's unlikely you're going to generate some major disaster. And you might. It happens sometimes to the best craftswomen in the world. We all have bad days and we all recover. You know what's worse than an actual creative disaster? Being so sure that you're going to create one that you never even get started. Don't be that woman.

Whatever way you look at it, you've got to practice. It's the only way. You've got to do some rubbish stuff to get better. So make a decision to get over it right now.

That old cliché really does have a point. It's the only way to get to almost perfect.

Because The Universe doesn't do perfect – you know that, right?

MAKE IT FUN

I have an idea, that just might help.

What if we were willing to see all of this as one big *playground*? What if we turned our attention to practice as *play?*

Fits quite nicely with *DROPPING HARD AND CHOOSING EASY,* doesn't it?

Practise, ugh, hard.

Play, ooh, fun.

Let's do that then.

Every day, you get to ask yourself this,

"What shall I play with today?" and,

"What can I make a total hash job of and have a good old giggle at?"

On more than one occasion, I've invited a client to actively make mistakes as a challenge. To produce rubbish work for me to see the next time we get together. It might be several pieces of absolutely appalling art (that have to be produced in 30 minutes or less) or a completely terrible strategy for their business or work.

Without fail, when I ask them to do this, they look at me like I am crazy. I can see them already making plans in their head to give me excellent art and breathtaking strategies.

They are completely willing to fail at the task I have actually given them in order to continue with their desire to create something perfect.

Even when they are given *permission* to do a terrible job, in fact, an *instruction,* that voice in their heads immediately goes to the tactics they could apply to not make it rubbish after all.

It's really important to notice when you're doing this. It is simply a form of self-sabotage. Your desire to be perfect, will keep you paralysed. Which is a bad, bad thing. Your desire to be perfect will keep you right where you are. Worrying about getting it wrong. All your attention goes to a thing that has never even happened and may never happen. Bonkers.

Notice when you're doing this. Take a deep breath in and screw up FAST.

One of my favourite teachers in the world is Brené Brown. You may have come across her TED talk on vulnerability. (If you haven't, now's the time. It's one of the most watched ever for a reason.) Early on in her writing career, she wrote a book called, 'The Gifts of Imperfection', and she used to teach elements of it in live workshops. Legend has it that she delivered one master stroke on a regular occasion. She would ask everyone to bring a beautiful journal to work with on the day of the session and at some point she would ask each participant to open their journal to begin to create.

Then comes the inevitable edge. The perfectionists in the room don't want to fill in that first piece of blank paper. They are afraid of ruining its pristine emptiness. Brené has it covered. To gasps in the room, she promptly resolves the issue for an unsuspecting perfectionist by walking up to their first page and scribbling on it with her pen. Ruining it.

I love the thought of this. Secretly, I'd be hoping it wasn't my journal. I have a feeling you would too.

Yet if we allow a moment to breathe, it's actually pretty funny and playful if you drop your adult for a minute and see it for what it is; a superb example of how much we can tie ourselves in knots about things that are not important at all.

So go forth and play. Notice where your fear of failure has you stay right where you are and be willing to mess things up in order to grow. Be bold, be playful. Practice for the joy of practicing and the excitement of improvement, accepting that you will make mistakes all of the time and in the knowledge that there is no such thing as perfection. Allow yourself to make rubbish things in service of developing your skills in the things that are most important to you...

Smile while you're at it – you're about to discover that mistakes are not the disaster you think they are, that building your skills is pure fun when you approach it playfully and willingly and that you can get better after all.

REFLECTION

4. *What have I not even started on because I'm so afraid of getting it wrong?*

(Some of you are going to have a belief that this isn't you at all. That you don't have a perfectionist bone in your body. I might have done too. Until I noticed this book has taken a LONG time to be completed and published. A ridiculous amount of time in fact. Especially when you consider I wasn't technically WORKING on it for most of that time...Look again).

5. *What is it I think will befall me if I make a mistake?*

For the next 7 days, play all out at the 'Creating Rubbish' game. Give yourself full permission to write crap blogs, make burnt cakes, put together ugly flower arrangements, speak terrible French. Every day do something terrible in service of getting started.

(Just to be clear, you fail at this game if you do it perfectly, your challenge is to do a BAD JOB. It's the only way you're going to learn that the sky doesn't fall down after all).

I commit to being completely rubbish at, and yet still doing <insert your stuff> for the next 7 days:

CHAPTER 7

PERMISSION TO DREAM

'THERE IS FREEDOM WAITING FOR YOU,
ON THE BREEZES OF THE SKY,
AND YOU ASK, "WHAT IF I FALL?"
OH BUT MY DARLING,
WHAT IF YOU FLY?'

ERIN HANSON

Kids are really good at dreaming (so much to learn from the kids).

Adults, not so much.

What we are really good at is *editing*.

Here's what I mean. A typical coaching conversation might go like this:

'What do you REALLY want right now?'

SILENCE.

You know why silence? Because we hardly ever allow ourselves to *speak* our deepest dreams. We edit them before they even become complete thoughts.

So, *'I really want to work three days a week',* comes out like this in conversation with your Crazy Lady:

YOU: 'I really want to work three days, need to think about how I ask for that...'

CRAZY LADY: 'Are you MAD? Who gets an actual job done in three days? NO-ONE is going to let you do that. For goodness sake, ask for something you have half a chance of getting'.

YOU: 'Ok, except I really think three...'

CRAZY LADY: 'Seriously woman, you are lethal. Are you trying to get fired? There's no point us having this conversation if you won't get realistic.'

YOU: 'OK, well I suppose I could work four days...'

CRAZY LADY: 'Hmm. Wonder if they'll go for that...how about a condensed week, then EVERYBODY wins.'

YOU: 'Right. I do five days work in four days. Well that's harder to say no to isn't it? Especially if I let them cut my salary a little bit. I'll ask for that then'.

Nice one.

You wanted three days.

You negotiated all the same hours in four for yourself, alongside a willingness to earn slightly less for your work without having a conversation with anyone.

Had you even noticed that you do that sometimes?

Permission to dream means that the seeds at least get put in the soil. Because if you leave them in the packet, there is zero possibility of them ever blossoming into a flower. You have already made the decision that they can't make it and you have denied them sunlight and water.

Play with this question for a moment (we'll come to it properly at the end of the chapter):

If you were to say all the things you REALLY want in your life, exactly as you want them, what would they be?

Note how quickly your brain moves some to one side as unreasonable, greedy, selfish, or any other of a range of excuses you've got going. They aren't allowed to be spoken, even in your own mind.

Interesting eh?

Am I saying you should throw all caution to the wind and go get them at all costs? Of course not.

I am saying it's time to be honest with yourself, it's time to talk about what you would love to create in your life so that it has even the smallest chance of becoming reality. Because in the not expressing, in the editing what you want and in the constant renegotiating down with yourself, you're doing an excellent job of ensuring with a cast iron guarantee that you cannot achieve your dreams.

I'm willing to bet that's not deliberate.

LIGHT BULB MOMENT

When I was a kid, I was wildly ambitious. I had a selection of dreams and I was crystal clear I could have all of them. It wasn't even a case of choosing. Why couldn't I just have exactly what I wanted?

My list went as follows:

1. To be a Missionary Doctor and go and heal the lepers in Africa (that didn't work out so well, on account of me being terrible at science).

2. To be a librarian, so that I could read books all day (a real librarian put me straight on this one. Apparently, that's not what you get to do. Which I still think is a bit ridiculous to be honest).

3. To be Captain of a TV show called, "It's a Knockout", so that I could have fun and be on telly (you had to be royalty to be a Captain when I was younger, so this was a bit of a non-starter).

4. To be Prime Minister, so that I could feed all the hungry people and stop all the wars (my politics professor put me straight on that one).

5. To write a book, so that I could join the band of people I most admired in life, authors, and say, *'I did it too'.*

6. Which I NEVER EVER SPOKE, to be a newsreader, chat show host or radio presenter.

Here's how they panned out for me:

- I didn't get to go and heal the lepers in Africa on account of the science thing. I did stay true to my childhood mission to help the third world though. Three years ago, I kicked off a fundraiser that raised over £100,000 to build a school in India. I will do more.

- In the end I didn't want to be a librarian. I achieve the real dream daily though. It would be unheard of for me to have less than three books on the go.

- I did have a bash at a local It's a Knockout. Turns out big inflatable costumes knock the wind out of you and are not even a little bit fun.

- I am not Prime Minister. You may have noticed this. Hmm. I took this dream out of the bag again recently to have another look. I want to create change in the world and I was curious – did I want to be in politics? I explored it very carefully. I spoke to local politicians and up and coming political members. I went to events at the House of Commons. I really dug deep. What I realised was that whilst I'm not sure I want to be a politician, I am sure I want more opportunity to work with the people who create change in the world. Which is what led me to open up Remarkable Women, our community for women who want to have a big impact.

- The book. Well here we are. Honestly? My third attempt. I have two beautifully written half books filed on my computer. Two books that I lost faith in and gave up on. So this time, I decided to make it easy (we just talked about that remember?) I decided to turn practice into play and to let go of all my perfection, not good enough, control freakery nonsense. I set myself 60 days to get a first copy manuscript done. If you're reading this, one way or another, I made it happen.

- The unspoken dream. Oh ladies, how's this for ironic? I worked for a TV company for *eleven years*. With an *unspoken dream* to be on TV. I did not enter the internal auditions to become a presenter, despite significant encouragement from a member of the Executive. I even won another competition to help my organisation come up with new programming ideas. Internally, I became known as 'One Take Danielle' because of my ability to speak to camera. I represented my organisation on a Consumer Affairs programme, which was frankly, Hell on Earth as I was pummelled for four and a half hours (for a three and a half minute slot) by a journalist for mistakes we had made. The PR team were delighted. I still never spoke my dream. Sometimes, my Crazy Lady tells me I am too old, mostly she tells me I am not good enough. Which, frankly, we already know is not true.

The good news is, here I am, co-running an organisation where I get to speak to camera all the time. I'm writing every week and focussing on building up women to go and have more impact in the world. I have unequivocal faith that some of those women will feed the hungry and heal the sick and influence some of the conflict. In that way, I will have pretty much realised every dream of my inner child, who, it seems, got quite a lot right.

So here's what's interesting. My inner child was bang on about the things I wanted. She's still right now I'm in my forties.

Most importantly, see this. When I denied my dream to be on TV, I sabotaged it every step of the way. I did it. Me. No-one else. I never let it be spoken. Even though I was in an environment where it could *easily* have been possible, I never gave it a chance.

HERE'S THE LESSON…

You must give your dreams permission to speak for them to have any chance at all of materialising. Without acknowledging them, without believing that there might be a glimmer of a chance that they could come true, well they just hide away in the dark, forgotten and unloved.

Even when all the signs say they could have some chance of growing into something special, it will be you who holds them back. It is only ever you.

So you want to stop that.

Permission to dream - all day long if that's what it takes.

It's another thing you need to practise.

And remember what we agreed in the beginning about your Crazy Lady?

This is not her time to shine.

You're just playing. With a piece of paper and a pen. Nothing dangerous going on here. Not a single thing to be afraid of.

Just a bunch of dreams getting their space in the world. Even Crazy Lady would love them to come true, underneath all her fear.

REFLECTION

1. *What are my unspoken dreams in the world? If I was willing to state them in all their glory, with not a single bit of editing, what would they be?*

2. *Check in: If I was completely unafraid of each and every one of them, do I really want to make them all happen?*

3. *For those that I do, how can I bring them to life by speaking about them more? Who will I share them with?*

CHAPTER 8

ASKING FOR HELP

'WHAT WILL PEOPLE SAY?'. THIS SENTENCE HAS KILLED MORE DREAMS THAN ANYTHING ELSE IN THE WORLD.'

UNKNOWN

Let's be very clear. You might think you are pretty good at this one. You need to do it more. Once you have learned how to do it more, you need to do it even *more*.

I cannot tell you how many stories I have from coaching clients who are addicted to going it alone, even when they have friends around them who have the willingness and the expertise to help.

LIGHT BULB MOMENT

A few years back, I spent the best part of a week on a leadership course learning how to ask for help. Yes, it's that important, I needed a whole week to learn it. Honestly, that wasn't long enough.

The group talked about it daily. We carried out a number of exercises showing just how rubbish we were at it and you know, I *completely* got it. Yes, I did. Back in the real world, I was going to *nail* this one.

Or not as it turned out.

At the very end of the week, I found myself leaving the main teaching room with my hands full of all the stuff I needed to take back to my room, the kitchen, or wherever they needed to go to be put away.

Books, a mug, a bottle of water, pens, a cardigan, you know, a lot of *stuff* for one pair of hands.

A friend opened the door for me, *'Can I help you with all that?'* he asked.

'No, no' says I, *'I'm absolutely fine. Not got far to go, I can manage it'.*

I walked about four steps away from him, struggling womanfully to hold everything without dropping it.

Then it dawned on me.

Good grief. If I couldn't even accept help when it was being offered to me for this tiniest of tiny things, what chance was there really that I had changed and would *ask* for help in the future?

And so I looked back,

'I don't need your help', I said, *'I've just realised, it would really be a lot easier if I took you up on your offer'.*

He smiled.

Somewhat brilliantly, he hadn't seen it either. Even though he had been in the same sessions as me all week.

Bonkers.

We struggle through an awful lot of stuff in life, often when there are people reaching out with open arms to help us.

And even though most of us love the feeling that comes from knowing we have helped other people (I'd go so far as to say it's one of the best feelings out there), our ability to ask for help, well, it leaves a bit to be desired.

A WHOLEHEARTED HANDFUL

A friend of mine recently modelled asking for help in a way that made me want to jump up and down and applaud her.

She was awaiting surgery. It came out of the blue and it really knocked her plans for the year out of orbit. So much so that if she didn't ask for help, she was going to have to do this pretty much on her own, as her husband needed to honour several critical commitments away from home.

Here she was, facing unexpected news and frankly, as most of us are when surgery is on the cards, a little anxious, frustrated, fearful and sad to be without her husband to support her. She needed help.

Her solution was to put together a What's App group of five or six friends that she called her 'Wholehearted Handful'.

The idea was that if she noticed that she needed anything, she could call on the group and with any luck, there would be enough people in the group that one would be able to step forward and respond to what she needed.

It could be anything - a visit, a hug, a phone call, a text of support, a trip to the supermarket to pick up some treats. Her theory was that it needed to be a group of people she trusted and loved and who she knew trusted and loved her and that if there were several of us in there, no-one particular person would feel obliged to step in every single time.

I was honoured enough to be invited into that group and I watched how it worked with delight. It was so good, I'm sharing it with you.

Yes, you could argue that these were pretty special women, because they stepped up in style. Yet, when I look back on that series of texts, I can see that everyone took a share in the helping and no-one ended up doing it all. I can't for one minute imagine that anyone felt put upon as a consequence of offering what they did to help and I felt pretty privileged to be able to do the small things I did to help make a difference.

That, my friends, is a brilliant example of *being the best leader of you in your life*.

Have a think about who your Wholehearted Handful might be in life - and before you start going all, *'Oh but I can't ask them, they don't have time to be around for me on the off chance I need help'* or whatever other nonsense that stops you from asking people for help, let me offer you this:

You really need to stop saying other people's 'No' for them.

Think about it for a minute. I'm holding you here consciously, because I know from my own experience, you're likely to be some time learning this. Truth? I had to learn again recently, that I really haven't got this nailed...

LIGHT BULB
MOMENT

I locked myself out of the house. With two poo bags and a dog on a lead. When I tell people this story, they think I end up fashioning some kind of rope with two poo bags to get in. This is not how the story goes. I just had two poo bags and a dog. And *no phone.* No means of getting back in and a husband literally the other end of the country running from Land's End to John O'Groats (as you do).

I spotted a man with a dog. *'Aha!'* I think to myself, *'I shall be smart and ask for help!'*

I noticed I felt a complete idiot as I confessed I had locked myself out and needed to call my husband (because that's the only number I know. Literally. More lessons there).

Luckily, John picked up the phone out on his run and I asked him to call Nic, my business partner, and let her know I was on my way (her flat is a forty minute walk away) so that she would stay in if she was planning to go out. I didn't know if he managed to get her because I didn't feel I could ask the guy whose phone I had borrowed to hang around for a couple of minutes for John to call me back.

No kidding. I had asked for help once, and that was enough thank you very much. I headed off to Nic's not knowing whether she was there or not.

That's not even where it ends. I then remembered we have an Airbnb lock box for our flat with three sets of keys in it. I didn't know the number (it's a hosted service) but I thought it would be on a message to a guest on my Airbnb account. So now I need to ask someone else if I can borrow their phone so I can go onto the internet.

I walked towards our supermarket and I jest you not...

I then hung around for ten minutes, deciding who looked like they would be willing to help me.

I literally discarded people who looked busy or cross or just, er, not quite right.

It gets worse.

Eventually I asked a kind looking man in a hard hat and a tool belt if he could help.

'Of course' he said and handed me his phone.

Completely flustered, I couldn't remember my password. I didn't want to hold him up (he is showing literally no signs of being bothered and is chatting and being friendly). After five minutes, I give him the phone back because I feel bad I have troubled him.

And then I walk the forty minutes to Nic's house (who is luckily there).

I truly hope you don't make the meal of it that I do sometimes, and I have enough client stories (including one of a normally brilliant woman humping a mattress up a flight of stairs even though two men offered to do it for her) to know that we're all at it one way or another.

ASK THE QUESTION

Deciding what people will say before you have even asked them, well that's just plain daft.

If you ask them they can say no anyway! Most of the time, people are happy to help. Even if they do say no, what's so bad about that? You can simply ask someone else.

So unless you're just allergic to the word, or you know you're going to take it deeply personally if they do say no (that's another book entirely), give them a chance to help you.

Imagine they enjoy the feeling of giving just as much as you do.

Why would you deny them that?

It doesn't have to be a Wholehearted Handful, it can be any version of asking for help you like.

What it does need to be, is one of the tools in your toolkit, so that when you realise you are struggling with something, you ask yourself this question:

'Who could help me with this right now?'

So simple really, right? You might even call it remarkably easy. If you're willing to try.

Then practise, practise, practise. I may have mentioned the need to do that before...

REFLECTION

1. *Where in my life do I consistently try to do things on my own when others could easily help me?*

2. *Is it a conscious choice that I don't ask? Do I even notice that I don't?*

3. *What are the things I make up will happen if I DO ask for your help?*

4. *Who could be in my Wholehearted Handful?*

YOUR THREE STEP PROCESS TO UNLEASHING YOUR BRILLIANCE

CHAPTER 9

WHAT ARE YOU GOOD AT?

'WE ASK OURSELVES, "WHO AM I TO BE BRILLIANT, GORGEOUS, TALENTED, FABULOUS!" ACTUALLY, "WHO ARE YOU NOT TO BE?" YOUR PLAYING SMALL DOES NOT SERVE THE WORLD.'

MARIANNE WILLIAMSON,
'A RETURN TO LOVE'

WARNING: Crazy Lady has NOTHING useful to say in this chapter.

Nothing.

Send her off for a walk. Just for a few minutes. Put her down.

Great. Now that's done, we're going to start here: with what we are good at.

Don't go getting all meek and coy on me. This character trait, ladies, does not serve us well. In fact, it's one of the core things at the heart of why women don't get promoted when they are more than ready for it.

Ask this question. In fact, ask this question a lot when you find yourself holding back.

'If no-one ever heard or saw what I am about to say, what gifts do I have that I am secretly DELIGHTED about? What do I know, deep down, regardless of what my Crazy Lady inner critic has to say, that I am really good at?'.

Write down the answers.

If you want to have an impact in the world and have the life you really long for, then you *have* to start owning this stuff. Today is the day we get started.

Make a list.

Here's mine:

- I have a talent for inspiring people

- I have a talent for giving people Rocket Fuel – the kind of momentum that has them inspired and in action

- I have a talent for making people believe in themselves

- I have a talent for making things easy and making things happen

- I have a talent for connecting the dots

- I have a talent for making people feel at ease

- I have a talent for speaking truths in a way that others can hear

- I have a talent for leading large groups of people through challenging times

- I have a talent for public speaking

- I have a talent for creating a vision that people want to believe in

- I have a talent for seeing what people are capable of

- I have a talent for learning – I am a brilliant Jack of All Trades

- I have a talent for connecting people

- I have a talent for helping people uncover their dreams

- I have a talent for helping others to find the words they want to say or write

And yes, *of course*, as I write this, my Crazy Lady is hovering nervously and going, '*You CAN'T WRITE THAT! They will*

HATE you.' She literally has her head in her hands saying, *'HOW CAN YOU BE THIS COCKY?'*

And notice, I am writing it anyway. Notice also that I have not said any version of the following:

'I think I'm pretty good at inspiring people. You might want to ask my team if they feel the same though <nervous laugh>. I mean, people have said that I am good at this and obviously, I'm not everyone's cup of tea...'

Or, *'Er, OK, what do I have a talent for? Erm. Gosh. Well, I wouldn't call it a talent as such, but you know, I'm not bad at making things happen. I think most people would say they would come to me if they wanted to get something done. It's probably a weakness really, you know, because people then think they can rely on you for everything and I'm not that good at saying no...'.*

I am also not saying what I do not have a talent for. There's plenty for sure.

For example, all the talents that are not listed above technically speaking. Which is a lot. Almost certainly millions of things when you think about it. So I'm hardly being cocky by mentioning the very small number of things I *am* brilliant at, am I?

Why, why, *why* would I want to spend time working out all the things I am *not*? Crazy Lady has that covered all day every day. She has a PhD in Things I am Crap At. This is apparently one of her unique talents.

Stick with yours.

Say them clearly and cleanly. Even if it makes you squirm.

I have a talent for...

Keep going till you run out. Write your unsayables. DO NOT EDIT because the Crazy Lady is hovering. At no point are you going to be forced to publish this on Facebook.

And you have more than two by the way. So just you keep going.

Finished? Good.

We'll be coming back to this. Don't be thinking we're done now.

For now though:

Round of Applause!

Big cheer coming from the back!

YOU HAVE A TALENT.

YOU HAVE MANY TALENTS.

YOU ARE TALENTED.

Thank goodness we finally worked that out. Took you long enough.

REFLECTION

1. *What am I really good at?*

2. *What am I not writing down in answer to the first question that secretly I want to?*

3. *What could change in my life and the life of others if I was willing to own my brilliance?*

CHAPTER 10

WHO ARE YOU REALLY?

'SHE REMEMBERED WHO SHE WAS
AND THE GAME CHANGED.'

LALAH DELIAH,
FOUNDER OF VIBRATEHIGHERDAILY.COM

I would hugely prefer it, for your sake, if you would take it from me that owning your talents is the easiest way to make an impact in the world.

I accept that you may want to find out the hard way.

I did, after all.

I focused on success and job titles first, fulfilment second.

This meant I got exactly what I focused on, er, success and job titles.

The thing is, it turned out they were not what I wanted *at all*.

I wanted *fulfilment*, and joy and *purpose*.

I also wanted security. I think most of us want that. And we readily persuade ourselves that it comes with success and job titles. It's not quite what you think it might be though. At least not in my experience anyway. But that's another story.

Turned out success and job titles didn't lead to fulfilment, joy and purpose at all. In fact, there was very little correlation indeed.

It's funny how so many of us are enticed by that road though. We're also great lovers of certainty. We should nip that in the bud now.

Here's what's absolutely certain in your life. It will end one day. That's it. The rest is probability, chance and action and still you are unable to guarantee a *single* thing. So you're chasing a truly daft thing there. In my experience, it's what has so many of us paralysed. Unable to take action. Even though we don't like where we are at that much at all, it's easier to stay there, uncomfortable and determined not to make things worse by moving forward. There's a way to live.

One life. One life. One life.

Got it yet?

Most of us never ask ourselves the question, 'Who am I?' and yet when we are willing to look into our biggest frustrations in life, they often show up because we are modifying our behaviour to fit in with others. We put our values and our deepest desires to one side, because we've decided we need to be someone else in order to maintain the status quo. It's a natural human desire to want to belong in the world and for women particularly, we find ourselves pleasing, helping, supporting in a way that often doesn't serve us. Or, we do whatever it takes to fit in. I believe that's why we find ourselves in a world where many of the most successful women have got where they are by learning to behave like the men in the room. They've learned how to be, 'one of the boys'. On the one hand, that's a smart tactic, if what you're aiming for is titles and success. When titles and success aren't in alignment with what we really long for in life, after a while, it starts to get pretty painful.

It might not be about titles and professional success for you either. It might be about being the success that comes with being a good daughter, or the perfect wife or mother. Whatever your definition of success, it's important to investigate whether you really mean to be the way you've chosen to be or whether it's a tactic to please others.

It's time to check in with who it is you're trying to please and why. It's time to explore whether who you're being in the outside world is truly aligned to who you are on the inside. Wherever there's not a match, there's an opportunity waiting impatiently to be noticed and transformed.

It always makes me smile when women come to me wanting to find a way to make the discomfort of not being their true selves go away without, well, changing to be their true selves. Not going to happen. Or at least, I've never seen it. What's also odd is that the fear, that is clearly quite real, can be difficult to articulate. We deeply long for the change and often, our fear of changing is fighting against that longing. We imagine we might lose our friends, our relationships, our status – without noticing that the status quo is what's causing us so much discomfort in the first place.

LIGHT BULB
MOMENT

The problem for me, is that I was 'quite good' at a lot of things. (Comes from my super talents – Jack of All Trades and my ability to learn). Turns out, this is not the same as *having a talent for something*.

How do I know this is not the same as talent?

Because a bunch of things I was quite good at hurt my brain. Not in a challenging, stretching, *'ooh, can I really do this'* kind of way... I experienced it more as *'these are days of my life I am never going to get back'*.

Being a Jack of All Trades meant that I could do lots of different things. Unfortunately, this also meant that when someone offered me a pretty new job title and some more money, my ego did a little twirly dance and accepted immediately, even though my soul (not my Crazy Lady) was shouting at the top of its voice, *'WHAT ARE YOU DOING?!'*.

All of this eventually ensured that I found myself in the most bonkers job of all. Running multi million pound complex technical change projects with a team of Project Managers and Analysts.

Let me be clear for a moment, just how bonkers that was:

I still don't know what an Analyst does.

Truth.

I mean, I know they are super clever people who can do things I can't. I'm pretty sure they would have a better description for themselves. You know, one that actually explains what they do and why.

And yet some brave person *put* ME *in charge* of these wonderful people.

I used to go home physically aching. We were getting the work done. Everyone was happy (this is likely to be a gross generalisation of course, and you know, we were doing well).

I was dying inside.

So I decided I would embark on the journey of discovering *'Who am I When I Don't Care What Anyone Else Thinks About Me?'*.

In a way this was a brave choice. Up until this point, I had built my career by learning to be exactly what everyone else wanted. It was a failsafe strategy. Except now I couldn't handle it any more. It was driving me insane. I had to do something.

I cared so much about feeling better that I simply had to stop caring about everyone else's opinion of me.

My particular path involved signing up for a ten-month intensive programme with eighteen strangers from all over the world. We met for one week, four times over the ten-month period.

I decided that since they didn't know me anyway and I already had friends, I could afford to take the risk. In fact, I spent so much on the programme, I couldn't afford to waste it. I showed up emotionally naked, as close to me as I knew how to be. I hid nothing.

To my surprise, I discovered that the hard-nosed style I had learned to adopt in business was almost non-existent when I wasn't interested in the opinion of others.

To my annoyance (now something I embrace), I discovered that whatever happened, everyone looked to me to be the leader. They saw me as someone with authority, capability and passion. (I did not like these words. I wanted something a bit more glamorous).

To my delight, I uncovered my heart. I discovered the pure joy in falling in love with every one of those people, many, many of whom I would never ever have allowed in my circle of friends in the past.

I discovered myself. Slowly, I fell in love with my talents. I fell deeply in love with my heart.

Things were about to change.

When I knew who I was, and when I discovered how much I liked that woman, the one I had been changing and adapting for everyone else for so long, *there was no holding her back.*

That turned out to be a very good thing indeed. For me and for everyone else in my life. I lived with excitement, passion, courage, unconditional love and belief in limitless possibility. Who doesn't want to have people in their lives coming from that place?

I realised I had spent so much time fitting in with what I thought was required and the ways I thought others wanted me to be in order that I could be 'successful' and 'belong' that I had completely lost sight of the things that only I brought to any situation. I was so busy fitting in, I had forgotten that there is no point to being unique in the world if all you do is hide it. I had forgotten to be excited by my dreams.

You know something else? I didn't even notice I was trying to fit in at such a high cost to myself. I thought one of my great gifts was reading a room and giving what was needed. If you had asked me did I care what anyone else thought about me, I would have laughed and said, 'of course not!' and yet, when I looked deep into my soul and heart and discovered all the treasures I was hiding, it was blatantly obvious that was what I was doing.

You see, I'm smart at kidding myself too. which may well be the same thing for you.

So before you go into the reflection, check in on whether there are people out there that you want to please, or who you hold back your brilliance from and check in on why. There might be great reasons for doing what you do and it's my job to have you sit with it for a while. To poke and prod and unsettle the way things are in service of you emerging bigger and bolder and truly living the life you were designed for. There will be gold in there for you, I guarantee it.

Because that amazing, super-charged, super-impactful woman, she's *inside* you. Waiting to get out - if only you would let her. And she's brave, strong and determined and resilient and just brilliant. All the things you're afraid you're not.

I know it feels scary. You've been running with these tactics for a while. You've set up a life where you believe that the reason people love you is because of the modifications you've made to have you fit in just perfectly.

Here's the thing. What if the world would love you *more* if you allowed the real you to show up? You'd never encourage your friends to live out of alignment with who they are. You'd be cheering them on to be their fullest most brilliant selves, to shine their light in their own unique way. That's great advice. You should listen to it.

Set her free. You've always had the key. Brave enough to turn it yet?

REFLECTION

1. *Whose opinion of me do I care about so much that I only bring some of me to the relationship?*

2. *Who would I be if I didn't care about what people thought about me or whether they liked me?*

3. *What would I be doing more of in the world if I truly didn't care how it looks?*

4. *What would people know about me that they never get to know now?*

CHAPTER 11

WHAT DO YOU STAND FOR?

'WHEN I GET TO THE END OF MY LIFE, AND I ASK ONE
FINAL, 'WHAT HAVE I DONE?', LET MY ANSWER BE,
'I HAVE DONE LOVE.'

UNKNOWN

Now we're trucking. You're really bringing it together now. You know *what you're brilliant at*, you're finally getting your head around *who* you are, and now we just want to add in the final piece of the puzzle - *what you stand for*.

To put it another way, as a leader, what's your mission in the world right now?

Let me just break that down a little. Firstly, notice I said what's your mission *right now*.

I did a tonne of work getting clear on my purpose - super clear and to be honest, it still evolves regularly, although it's always grounded in the same theme. When I talk to people about purpose, my sense is the question feels important, critical and often, way too big to even know where to get started. Which means we don't.

The good news is, I have a shortcut for you.

Brian Johnson, of the somewhat awesome, www.optimise.me, takes purpose to its simplest form.

He suggests that we are on this planet to *use our gifts to the best of our ability in service of others*.

He goes onto say that life is simply a series of missions. As we find ways to use our gifts to the best of our ability, we uncover missions, we complete them and we move on to the next one.

Sometimes we have more than one mission going at a time (for example, part of using your gifts to serve others may be to be the best parent you know how to be, whilst also completing a second mission that is how you generate impact in what you choose to do in your professional life).

I love this concept. It takes so much pressure off working out one big thing and simply has us out in the world offering up the things we do brilliantly in the best way we know how.

FINDING YOUR MISSION

We've already covered what you're brilliant at, because you need to know what your gifts are in order to use them to the best of your ability.

Next, you have to be willing to *own* them as yours. If you don't own what you are brilliant at, there's no way you're going to be able to do your very best in whatever it is you have chosen, when your own mind is telling you to hold back, not show off, play small.

And the mission?

It becomes whatever you choose it to be.

Choose though - consciously and carefully.

Should you be working for an organisation, don't mistake it for *what they want the outcome to be for them*. With all due respect, that's *their* mission, it's not yours.

If this is the organisation you want to contribute to, you can however, find a mission that works for them and is in alignment with their mission.

LIGHT BULB
MOMENT

Back in my corporate days, my personal mission, as a leader of 10,000 people, was to create an environment where people loved what they did and had the freedom to shine every day. I wanted them to be connected to their own significance, brilliance and purpose. I worked consistently on that for four years. I used my talents to inspire others to believe they were capable of more. I used them to create a vision that people believed in and I used them to make it seem possible, easy, fun, rewarding and meaningful.

Honestly? I didn't really care about shareholder value and profit. Truly. It wasn't a secret.

What I wholeheartedly believed was that if I created an environment where people loved what they did and were allowed to shine every single day, we would create exceptional results. I believed that with every ounce of my being and I chose to live by it every day.

I loved that work. There was nothing more fun for me than giving my attention to how others could be brilliant.

I let someone who loved numbers keep an eye on them. He was doing what *he* loved and shining every day. I built a team who all focused on the areas of the organisation that they loved and as a collective, we had everything covered.

And lo and behold, those numbers magically appeared. With me focusing on my strengths, staying true to what was really important to me, and being crystal clear about what I stood for, turning as much of my attention as was physically possible to the things I could do really well.

STILL NOT BUYING IT?

It's entirely possible you are looking at my mission at that time (I have another one now, it's even bigger – you'll find out about it at the end of this book) and thinking, *'there she goes again, I don't want to do that kind of thing, this isn't for me after all...'.*

Stop. Right. There.

Let me remind you again. I'm *illustrating* with my examples. Whatever you choose to do in the world is what's right for you. I'm inviting you to get clear on what that is - to align your talents and your ability to own them with what you can create in the world.

As you explore that, it's important you know this.

For several months now, I've been interviewing 'successful women' on whether they choose to live into their full potential in the world. What I've discovered is, on the whole, they're not.

They're doing what I did. Chasing job titles and money.

Worse yet, they know it.

When I ask them what they would be doing if they were allowing their full potential to be realised, they all talk about wanting to make a difference in the world. Getting away from money and into making change.

They *all* talk about it. There's a small bunch *doing* it and the rest are *talking* about it. They are all quite brilliant women and far too many are being held back by their fears.

IT'S DEEP INSIDE US

We all want to make a difference, in our own way. Some of us want to bring up the next generation to be exceptional. Some of us want to create community on our street or our town or village. Some of us want to change the world.

Every single one of these is a valid mission.

Your deepest desire for change is valid.

So sit down for a moment and give yourself the freedom to dream. Look at those strengths and your own unique design and line them up to the things you really want to create in your world.

Then look at how you can start creating that *now*.

You don't have to leave the job you've got or throw caution to the wind. You have to show up as YOU. Living from that place. The one where you know you have gifts and you accept they are for sharing.

Make this *easy*. How can you serve in the world with your unique combination of gifts?

Oh, and by the way, should Crazy Lady have popped up to remind you you're not that good at anything. Yes you are. You have more gifts than that

Tons more.

Remember that list of your talents?   Now's the time to go back and add more.   It's clearly not long enough. Ask your friends if you've gone all humble again, because in this instance, that humility is fear rearing its head again.

Make this easy on yourself and let's get cracking with that mission. You're going to love it.

REFLECTION

1. *Now I know what I'm brilliant at, if I wasn't afraid, how would I use those gifts in the world to make a difference to others?*

2. *Standing where I am, right now, how could I offer my gifts in my current circumstances?*

3. *What excites me most about this? How do I get started?*

There's your mission, right there. RIGHT NOW.

One day it may be complete. And you might start another one. If you really want to dream big, write the big dream below. One sentence, no ifs and buts, simply let it breathe. So you can see where you're really heading.

For now let's get cracking with the first one. You'll be amazed at where it might lead you.

MY BIG DREAM...

MAKING THINGS HAPPEN: ACTION, ENERGY AND INSPIRATION

CHAPTER 12

JUST GET MOVING

'ONE DAY OR DAY ONE. YOU DECIDE.'

UNKNOWN

Crazy Lady gets a bit freaked by missions. They overwhelm her. Which often means she does a marvelous job of becoming the world's most effective blocker. She really is incredibly talented, relentless and tenacious.

There she is wringing her hands nervously, bemoaning how everything could go wrong and every time you go to make a move, she yells, *'STOP! You don't know how to DO this!'* and if we're not very careful, we hear her nervous cries and we reply, *'Yes, you're right - I better sit down and think about it one more time'.*

It's a vicious circle. There is no way out of it. The task at hand becomes so overwhelming that you simply never get started. There is always something you don't know, someone else who could give you an opinion, more numbers that could be crunched, other options that could be checked out.

That's why this book is subtitled, 'How to get out of your own way and unleash your brilliance'. I want you to get into the practice of noticing how it is almost always *you* holding you back. Once you see that, you can have a good laugh and move on. Create motion. Make it *easy*.

THE SMALLEST STEPS CREATE UNIMAGINABLE MOMENTUM

The only tasks in life that are impossible to complete are the ones we never start.

All we have to do is get started. With imperfect action. With *something*.

The way we do that in the beginning is to focus on the *very first step*. And then the one after that and then the one after that, until one day we find we are indeed running at full pace and we look back and think, *'Wow, how did I get here?'* and we realise we're not worrying about it anymore, because in taking one step at a time, it all got a little less overwhelming and a little more possible.

You've got to break it down into small easy steps.

The great thing about one tiny step is it is never scary. It's always doable and simple.

If I had written on my to do list today, 'Finish my book', I can absolutely guarantee that I would have done *every single other thing* on my list before opening up the manuscript and getting moving.

Why? I think it's human nature to like to feel we have accomplished something in a day and so sometimes it feels necessary to tick off a few things in my head or on a bit of paper to consider I have been productive.

Or maybe, really, it's this.

'Finish my book' is WAY TOO OVERWHELMING. Ridiculously overwhelming.

Why would I even think of starting such a mammoth task when I could just write a blog or send some emails? Not a chance I'm going to turn my attention to this one, thank you very much. Even my Crazy Lady, who is on the whole fairly well tamed, is going to have a field day with that one.

So what I actually have on my to-do list is this:

'One Page'.

That's it.

It says the same thing every single working day.

All I have to do to take it off the list is type out One Page. Even if it's a complete load of rubbish.

THAT is getting in motion.

Before we get going on creating your easy steps, here's a couple more examples so that you can see just how simple you can make things:

- When I gave myself the mission of 'creating an environment where all 10,000 people will love what they do and have the chance to shine every day' (try putting that on your to-do list for something you'll never get started), step one was to go and visit every site and share my mission with them. Just those words. Technically, I wasn't doing anything at all to move us forward. Except I was of course - I was sharing my thoughts, checking they were valid, *whilst* making a public commitment. I was also making sure Crazy Lady was clear we were going to be on this road for a while, whether she liked it or not.

- For a client of mine, her most overwhelming task was that she needed to completely overhaul her website. It had been preying on her mind for months. Step one? Take down the existing one and put up an 'under exciting new construction' notice. It probably only took about ten minutes. The most important thing was, she was off. Out of paralysis and moving and feeling a lot better about herself.

DO IT NOW

Do the thing that takes your mission forward before ANYTHING else. Make it the first thing you do.

I learned this one the hard way.

LIGHT BULB
MOMENT

When we set up our business, Somebody Inside, it took me almost 18 months to realise I had created quite the perfect system for playing small. I had it well and truly nailed. My whole day was so full of a million very important things to do that I never set aside any time whatsoever to do the things I really dreamed of. I was the busiest woman in the world doing the sum total of absolutely nothing.

I decided to take stock of all the things I was doing and assess whether they really made a difference or not. Once I had it all written down and I had had a good old laugh at myself, I made one simple decision. The first half hour of every day would be in action on a thing that really mattered to me on my mission to create a world where women have more impact. I turned my attention to writing this book and to contacting just one person per day that I wanted to be in connection with, to having one single conversation.

Everything changed. Before I knew it, the momentum and traction on my work in the world had changed entirely. The things that used to be on my to-do list were discarded – it didn't take long to realise I didn't need to do them at all, or at the very least, I could do them a lot less often than I used to. It was an exciting revelation.

Once again, I had been getting in my own way. And the way out, well it was remarkably easy. One simple shift in the first half hour of my working day and the whole system for playing small fell apart beautifully.

Don't you love it when that happens?

The way out of the overwhelm is to pick one thing and do it right now and then to get up tomorrow and go again. To show up consistently and persistently every day with your focus on the one thing that you want to create or change.

We're often out there looking for a silver bullet. The thing that will magically create significant progress in our lives.

This is it.

I wish it had more pizazz for you and that we could get the fireworks out and celebrate together. I wish I had found out sooner. I wish it was a shiny revelatory insight that might have you leap up and say, 'Yes! I get it now!'.

I wish that you can see beyond its brilliant simplicity and imagine just what might be possible if you took one small step every single day in the direction you most desire. It really is all it takes.

Break it down.

Pick the most obvious first step (make it as small as possible).

Do it before you do anything else.

Repeat tomorrow.

And the day after.

Simples.

REFLECTION

1. *What's the thing you've been putting off for ages or talking about for years and have never quite got started on because it just seems too big or too hard?*

2. *What's one easy step that you can do today that will take you one small step ahead of where you are right now?*

Map out one small action for the next seven days. Put it in your diary and enjoy ticking it off before you do anything else.

MONDAY:

_____

TUESDAY:

_____

WEDNESDAY:

_____

THURSDAY:

_____

FRIDAY:

_____

SATURDAY:

_____

SUNDAY:

_____

CHAPTER 13

STOCK UP ON INSPIRATION

'STICK WITH THE PEOPLE WHO PULL THE MAGIC OUT OF
YOU AND NOT THE MADNESS.'

UNKNOWN

We have this really weird habit of not looking for inspiration until we have drained ourselves of every bit that we have. You know what I mean, I know you do.

You push, push, push, thinking, *'just one more day of this and everything will be fine'*, you work the long hours, you suck up work you hate in service of some future imaginary payoff, you keep saying yes to jobs your partner or your kids want you to do and then one day, BOOM!

Exhaustion. Empty. There you are, on the floor, all out of inspiration.

In fact, you're all out of joy.

The first time we do this to ourselves, we trick ourselves into believing it will never happen again.

It doesn't quite work out that way. We're soon back into our old rhythm, persuading ourselves that we can fit more in, do more, put off meeting *our* needs until tomorrow.

CHOOSE SOMETHING DIFFERENT

It's a choice to get out of old patterns and into something new and better. We need to nurture and nourish our joy for it to stay vibrant and alive. We want to love and tend to it like the precious gift that it is.

A great way to do that is to find our sources of inspiration.

If you really do want to be the best leader of you, then you want to be filled with inspiration for as many days of your life as possible.

INSPIRED action is very different to regular, everyday action. It has a passion, a drive and an energy that keeps it in motion. With very little effort at all, it simply BELIEVES in what it is creating. (This means the Crazy Lady inside has a day off. Another very good thing for the two of you.)

Of course, we all have days when that just doesn't work out for us. So, what we need is a bank of places, people and things that we can turn to in order to lift our spirits, offer new ideas and frankly, simply cheer us on our way.

We want to *fuel* our body and mind with:

- Ideas that excite us;
- People and teachers that challenge and stretch us;
- People that love and encourage us;
- Places that ground us;
- Movement that energises us;
- Food that nourishes us;
- Sources of laughter and fun;
- Mental practices that keep us in flow;

And we want access to that fuel in some form *every single day*.

In fact, for the first time in your life I suspect, permission to be GREEDY. Really go for it when it comes to the Inspiration Larder.

THE INSPIRATION LARDER

The Inspiration Larder is what prevents the tough days from lasting for a long time, it is what picks us up on the grey days and what has us flying even higher than we would otherwise on the great days.

This is the toolkit that means we never have to do it on our own. (By the way, your story about having to work it out yourself, that's a daft one too. Everyone's life is the product of the things that have gone into it. None of us live in a vacuum.)

Make the most of everything that's on offer! It's how you bring the ingredients together that will make your Inspiration Larder unique to you.

We'll start with your mornings...

THE MORNING RITUAL

In order to get you in the habit of using your Inspiration Larder every day, I'm going to suggest you start with a Morning Ritual.

By that, I mean, having a specific way of starting your day, in order to give you the best start possible.

(Right now, I can hear the mums groaning. *'IS SHE FOR REAL? Have you ever been in my house in the morning?'*).

Bear with me. There's something in here for you too. I'm not going to ask you to make green smoothies and meditate for four hours. Although, knock yourself out if that's your thing.

In the simplest terms the reason we create a Morning Ritual is to ensure that our day starts with *something* that inspires us. It's a message to the next 24 hours that we intend to have a great day, thank you very much and we're starting right away.

Here's what my own Morning Ritual looks like:

First there's a 20 minute meditation and 20 minutes of journaling, which essentially means I spend some time writing about what I'm looking forward to in the day and what I'm committed to creating. Essentially, it's a way of waking my mind up to the day ahead and giving it a sense of purpose.

Next, a 20 minute walk with my dog Scruffy in the fresh air taking time to notice what's around me (OK, I live in Scotland, so by fresh air I often mean howling wind and rain, but I promise you, even in the rain I'm blessed with a very special view that definitely counts as places that ground me). This is followed by my very favourite breakfast smoothie recipe or two poached eggs and avocado on toast (food that nourishes me).

On many days, that walk with Scruffy is with my husband John, also providing me with an extra bonus of people who love and encourage me.

When I used to need to drive for an hour to work each morning, my morning ritual was different. My journaling moved to the evenings (some days not at all) and in the morning, I would use my travel time to stock up on joy, either putting on some of my favourite music and singing full blast all the way to work (sources of laughter and fun) or listening to a podcast with one of my favourite teachers (ideas that excite us and teachers who challenge and stretch us).

So that's *five* sources of inspiration before I even got to work. And not a bit of effort or trying or lengthy preparation involved in a single one of them (bear with me mums, I'm wholly aware you're probably still sighing and about to give up on me).

This is all very different indeed to how my mornings used to be...

They went something more like this - see if you recognise the pattern:

7.30am: Alarm goes off.

I slap the snooze button frustratedly. I *hate* alarm clocks.

7.40am: Reluctantly decide will need to wake up. Look at email. And Facebook. Look at email again. And Facebook. Continue in this mode for ten minutes at least.

7.50am: Look at the time and realise I don't have much of it. Leap out of bed angrily and into the shower muttering about alarm clocks. Hot water puts me in slightly better mood.

8.00am: Look in wardrobe. Hate all the clothes. Try on several outfits. Settle for one I always wear. Look at myself disapprovingly and sigh as I leave the bedroom.

8.10am: Dry hair and put on make up. On good days John brings me peppermint tea. Sometimes I even remember to say thank you.

8.25 am: Grab cereal bar. Check Facebook and Email. Give John a kiss and leg it out of the door.

8.27 am Get in car. Realise have conference call to dial into. Dial in two minutes late like everyone else. Listen to all the people arriving to said call and apologizing for being late. Drive to work half listening whilst sighing inside, knowing that this is precious minutes of my life I will not get back. Fail to notice when I am asked questions. Pretend reception is dodgy.

9am: Arrive at work. Set about the business of inspiring people.

Ah.

Really? Inspiring people when that was the way I started my morning?

Tired, grumpy, stressed and a bit hacked off. An excellent recipe for being a terrible leader of me, and bad news for those who worked for me too, for at least the first hour of the day.

SET YOURSELF UP FOR A GREAT DAY

Somewhere along the way, we have learned to discard that precious time in the morning. For many of us it has become the time we have to run around getting ready for whatever it is we plan to do for the rest of the day. We have forgotten it is our time to choose new ways.

And now I'm offering it to you as the way you *fire up* your day.

Simply choose a brighter start to the morning. If your kids drive you bonkers first thing, choose *something, anything* in the inspiration larder that could work for you and make sure it is a part of your morning.

Choose to laugh with the kids - because it's YOU who is modelling to them that mornings are a bit stressful and rubbish.

Put on your favourite music and play it while you find the missing shoe.

Sit down and have a tasty and nourishing breakfast with your significant other.

Hide in the bathroom for five luxurious minutes of breathing. OK, two.

Open the windows and breathe in the fresh air.

Whatever you choose, set up your day with an injection of inspiration. Fill it with joy.

I don't care what your morning ritual is. I care that it starts your day well. Think of the Inspiration Larder as a pick and mix if you will. I've given you the categories, you choose your specific ingredients.

Get a Morning Ritual. And once you've got it, stick to it. Keep the list short. It needs to be manageable and doable. We're all about easy, right?

Be honest with yourself. If you know deep in your heart, that you are never ever going to incorporate a meditation practice for more than two days, don't put it into the ritual. This is about what sets you up well, what would give you an energising and invigorating start to your day. It's not about having a ritual that you think I would approve of (because I know some of you are going there), it's about giving yourself a great start to the morning.

Only you know what that looks like.

REFLECTION

1. *What could I do to really start my day well?*

Pick just ONE thing for tomorrow.

Do it for seven days at least before bringing in anything else.

M ☐ T ☐ W ☐ T ☐ F ☐ S ☐ S ☐

Then build up your menu, one by one until you have
a morning rhythm you would never compromise.

2. Week 2, I'll be including:

3. Week 3, I'll be including:

4. Week 4, I'll be including:

CHAPTER 14

INSPIRING IDEAS AND THE PEOPLE WHO TEACH THEM

'THE BEST TEACHERS ARE THOSE WHO SHOW YOU WHERE TO LOOK BUT DON'T TELL YOU WHAT TO SEE.'

UNKNOWN

The amazing thing about this digital world we live in, is that we have access to information on just about *everything* you can imagine. I mean a friend of mine who is into crafting told me there's more than you can imagine to be learned about the right type of glue to use in different scenarios, for example.

Get out of here! A whole world of information on types of glue?

Actually, how brilliant is that? And that's just one topic.

Now that you know not to be comparing your early work to that of the gurus (remember my point on Star Wars and George Lucas back in Chapter 9?), you can listen to what they have to say and learn from their experience.

There are so many ways to get hold of information on the topics that interest you.

It's time to become an explorer.

FINDING YOUR TEACHERS

The word teacher might be having an impact on you before we even start. Notice it and let it go. I'm talking about that one teacher you really loved. The one whose class you couldn't wait to get to, because she always had something ready to inspire and excite you. We're looking for more of her.

In the beginning it might feel a bit overwhelming to know where to start and you will almost certainly have to do some filtering. This could easily have you back off quickly. You might listen to ten minutes of one podcast and go, *'what a load of rubbish, even I know more than that!'*.

Isn't that great? You've already realised you know more than you thought you did! Bank that realisation with a smile and then try another one.

Stay with it until you start to uncover the gems that fire you up. Trust that very soon you will be able to discern between what's inspiring for you and what's not. When you find your sources, trust them, turn back to them and in time, expand them.

Once you find your people or person, hang around for a while. Soak up their stuff before you go searching for more.

I promise you will know when you find them. They are the ones that have you longing for more every time you listen to them, watch them or read their writing. They are giving you the information you need to hear, in a way that resonates with you and excites you. They are providing new insights to things you have been thinking about for a while and they get your creative juices flowing.

They are offering you a path to expand your learning. They do more than pass on information, for you, they are *inspiration*.

Become part of their tribe. Soak up what they have to say. Get your learning on and watch how your own creativity flows as you learn new angles and new skills.

Notice the way you're starting to bring the things they teach you into conversation more and more and how those conversations are sparking up new insights. Notice your willingness to start practicing whatever it is they are teaching you. Get stuck in and play all out.

Unless you are a world genius, there will always be people who have done more thinking around a subject than you. Even if you *are* a world genius (major round of applause for owning that label), there will always be people who are investigating different angles than yours, who have done more detailed thinking on certain things, who can *show you the next step*.

Even as adults, we need teachers, to expand our mind and to keep us inspired. The good news is as adults, we get to *choose* our teachers, which means we don't need to sit at the back doodling in our books any more. We can sit *right at the front* where you can see and hear best. We become active eager learners, because this is good stuff and we want to take it in.

Use the time you have well. This is fun after all, it's fueling you up with energy and possibility. Download podcasts for the train ride, play them in the car, in the bath, or wherever. That time you spend scrolling social media out of sheer boredom, swap it for *this* stuff.

Think about it. You have access to leading thinkers and emerging entrepreneurs in every topic the world has been able to think of. It has *never* been easier to access information on anything from fitness to cooking to archaeology to parenting to comedy to crafting to relationships.

You name it, it is there. Even better, a whole bunch of it is free.

Make it a practice in your life.

If you're reading this and thinking, *'how boring, what is she on about?'*, you just haven't found your people yet. They are out there.

I can also pretty much promise you won't find them lurking in your professional membership magazine in case you were wondering...

This is your learning playground, you follow and learn from the people who excite YOU. Get out there and find them.

Oh, and have fun doing it.

LIGHT BULB
MOMENT

Let me share with you how I got started finding my current Inspirational Learning Network (I made that up by the way. Capital Letters make things official right?).

Cheesy though this may sound, for me it was the book, Eat Pray Love.

I know. Some of you are probably slapping your forehead right now. Really, not my usual path of discovery - a best-selling book with Julia Roberts on the cover (yep, I read it that late, resisted it for that long. Also, I love Julia Roberts and that movie, it's a big no for me).

I put off reading it for ages. Then one day I sat down and found myself lost in a story that really spoke to me.

The important thing for you to understand though, is that this story led to other things:

- It led to me following Elizabeth Gilbert on Facebook.

- It led to me listening to her Magic Lessons podcast, which then opened up the world of podcasting.

- It led to her recommending other writers like Brené Brown (who I happen to think is a genius).

- And when I started following Brené Brown, she started recommending other writers and teachers, and I started to follow them.

Before I knew it, I had this *never-ending* source of inspiration to tap into. A selection of podcasts and writers who made me curious about life and who offered me any number of different ways to rethink my own dilemmas and challenges.

It maybe took a year or so to realise how to really mine all the content out in the world.

Then I wanted friends to explore this stuff with. So I started a non-fiction book club with a bunch of inspiring women (another way to get a Wholehearted Handful together, that we talked about in Chapter 8) and they started to put books into the group I would *never* have read otherwise (including some that broke my brain).

Start your treasure hunt now and make it easy.

It's time to fire up *your* curiosity:

- Sign up to the blogs of one writer you enjoy.

- Notice who they recommend and get curious about why.

- Start reading the book section in magazines that you read regularly – order the books that most interest you (the subject really doesn't matter, go with your instinct).

- Ask for recommendations from people you know – books, writers, podcasts, films, whatever you know works for you.

- Explore the vast resource that is available on TED.

- Set up a group of friends who want to talk about this stuff too – you only need to meet every six weeks or so.

See, it really is that simple...

REFLECTION

1. *What's one book on my kindle / bedside table or Podcast I've saved or TED Talk I stored to 'listen to later' that I'm willing to commit to engaging with in the next seven days?*

2. *What subjects do I know I'd like to learn more about? Where can I start?*

3. *Who have I heard of that I'd like to explore further?*

4. *Or, who could I ask for a recommendation?*

CHAPTER 15

PEOPLE THAT ENCOURAGE AND STRETCH US

'NEVER COMFORT ME WITH A LIE.'

UNKNOWN

You're probably thinking, *'Hang on a minute, what's the difference between these and the ones who inspire us?'* It's a fair question.

The people that encourage and stretch you are in your life *right now*. They are very specific and special people - the ones that kindly and lovingly call you out on your negative thinking. They are the ones who speak and you sit up and listen. They aren't necessarily your best friends. They are the people that help you grow every time you spend time with them.

These people in your life are an exceptional mix of:

- Challenging and supporting

- Encouraging and realistic

- Ruthlessly compassionate with their insight

- Empathetic, not sympathetic

These are the people you go to when you *really* want help. When you want to see if there is something beyond the story you are running over and over again in your head and move forward in a healthy way.

You go to them because you know they won't collude with you. They won't offer you tissues and say *'there, there'*. They don't ever see you as broken or crazy and in fact, most of the time, they believe in you even more than you do yourself. That's why they call things out when you're letting the Crazy Lady run the show.

Those of you who have one of these in your life already, know *exactly* who I'm talking about. I'm willing to bet your time with them is precious indeed. We *need* these people in our lives. They shine a light on the path so that we can get moving.

LIGHT BULB
MOMENT

If you can't quite work out the kind of person I'm talking about, let me tell you about one of mine.

I hit the jackpot.

She happens to be my business partner in Somebody Inside, Nic. I get a good old boost of honest love pretty much every day of the working week. Sometimes the weekend too.

There was a time in my life, in the big corporate career days, where I ran it to the wire. I had this habit of working as hard as I possibly could, burning the midnight oil, giving up all sense of self-care and exercise, eating crappy food, packing in meetings, travelling all over the place with no rest. I was doing a good job but everyone could see it wasn't sustainable. So there would be points in my life where I would just hit a brick wall.

Smack.

And then I would have no choice but to rest and recover.

It was a pretty stupid strategy. Some of you are undoubtedly familiar with it already. You have one just like it.

I credit this strategy completely with 12 years of back pain, culminating in a disc prolapsing twice over a six month period.

The second time it went was the end of the line. The nerve in my leg had also become severely damaged as a consequence of the disk leaking. The best way I can describe it to you is that it was as though someone was holding a flame to my leg.

I had never experienced pain like it. I was in Spain in a motorhome, desperately waiting for morning to come so I could get to hospital with not a single second of relief.

Morning finally came, and after pumping me up with bags of IV drugs, the hospital said I could fly home for surgery. Three friends stepped up to support me while John drove the van back. They were all amazing. Nic was one of them.

Surgery followed two weeks later, after which I couldn't sit for more than half an hour for weeks. I was consigned to bed for around 22 hours a day.

Quite brilliantly, after about three days post-surgery (because obviously even I knew I needed to have *some* recovery time), I was still clinging onto the idea that I would continue to work with my laptop propped on my knees.

Nic came to see me and I gave her my usual cheery nonsense about how fine I was and that it really was time to get back to work.

She looked at me with the saddest eyes and said, *'I don't know how to help you any more, Danielle. I don't know what it will take for you to make the change your body is begging for. You have to stop playing at this'.*

BOOM.

THAT is people who encourage and stretch us look like.

They are the people who love us so much that they will not collude in our story. The people who look us in the eye and tell us *what we already know* in a way that we have to hear and receive it.

We *really* need these people in our lives. Without them we persuade ourselves all kinds of nonsense. We play small.

If you have one or more people like this in your life, then you're on your way.

If you haven't, it's time to get on the lookout.

Here are two ways to make sure you introduce one of these brilliant characters into your life: you can either look for a mentor that is in your personal or professional circle already, or you can hire a coach.

START WITH WHO YOU KNOW ALREADY

When you read the description of the kind of person that stretches and encourages us, did anyone that you know of come to mind? If yes, it's time to see if they would be willing to spend more time with you.

Be clear that you don't require much of it and you do need to ask whether they have the space, time and desire to support you. These people can have a big queue of people who want more of them.

If they are at work, ask them if they would be willing to mentor you. If they say no, ask if they can recommend someone else who thinks like they do.

For goodness sake, just ASK.

Remember what I said about not saying people's no for them? Part of being the best leader of you is that you put out there what you want. The worst that can happen is that they say no. And since you don't have them in your life right now anyway, nothing has actually changed as a consequence. Even if they don't say yes immediately, you will be in their subconscious. You never know when the time might arise in the future when they appear with a recommendation or an introduction that turns out to be just the thing you need. Get on their radar.

Ask.

Ask.

ASK.

I'm saying this a lot for a reason.

I know some of you are squirming. Check out why. It's easy for me to say, *'what have you got to lose?'* and yet if your Crazy Lady is running the show, she seems to think all kinds of things might happen.

However, if you check in on what disaster it is you do think will befall you, it usually involves the sound of someone saying, *'I'm sorry, I really am not able to commit to that right now'*.

For some reason this goes through the Crazy One's filter and is responded to as follows, *'Good grief, you've made a complete FOOL of yourself now. She is going to laugh about you to literally EVERYONE she meets, for, like, ever.'*

So let me remind you again, much as your Crazy Lady is a passenger all of the way on this journey of your life, she has a PhD in Exaggeration and a Masters in Panic. Plus if she was to take an exam on the accuracy of her predictions, she would *fail miserably*. So, smile, thank her for her opinion and ask anyway.

This is about creating the life you long for, and lady, I promise you, there's no Prince on a White Horse coming to line it all up for you.

HIRING A COACH

A simple and hugely effective way to find someone who stretches and encourages you is to hire a personal coach. This way, you are contracting with someone to believe in you until you are ready to do it for yourself. Coaches do the job they do because they inherently believe in people and they are passionate about using their skills to enable you to have the life that you long for but can't quite see how to make it happen.

It's their job to love you, believe in you, hold you accountable and help you discover the path that inspires you.

Go on a search to find someone who most resonates with you.

Essentially you're looking for someone that will give you a different perspective, who will always believe in you and who will make sure that you don't go off hiding in a corner. Only you know what kind of person that is for you. Be discerning. When you meet them, you will pretty much know immediately. Don't settle for anyone who doesn't give you a 'Hell, Yeah!' feeling. Anyone who falls into 'maybe' is the right coach for someone else and not for you.

Hire the one you really want and meet them regularly, for at least six months. You're looking to get traction here.

After six months, you might find you want some space to explore on your own and you'll meet them a little less or you may find that you want to have a continued relationship. It's always your choice. A good coach isn't going to push themselves on you. They don't need to. That's part of who they are. A great coach is worth every penny. If you're willing to get out of your own way, you will transform your life.

LIGHT BULB
MOMENT

I've had a coach in my life every year for the last 10 years. It all started with my organisation wanting to teach leaders like me to coach others.

Most of us had no idea what coaching was. So we were given an experience of it first.

I met up with an internal guy I vaguely knew who had been coaching for a while. I shared with him the bitterness I felt towards my boss at the time and how I felt our relationship had gone down the pan. I had been pretending it wasn't bothering me, the truth was, it was festering away beautifully.

Working with him over the course of just 90 minutes (and crying a bit, because 1) I always cry in coaching and 2) crying is just a release of emotion in case you hadn't noticed and not in fact, a shamefully embarrassing thing to do in public), I had a massive breakthrough.

I was hurting so much because it wasn't like me to be caught up with so much resentment. I didn't like being in relationships that were sticky and crunchy. I was disappointed with *myself*, because out of my resentment had come a number of actions from me that were simply out of alignment with who I was.

Even though I had been blaming my boss and had developed a great skill in noticing all the things he did 'wrong', the real issue for me was that I didn't like who I had become as a consequence.

Without coaching I would never have seen that.

The next day I met with my boss and we talked. By the end of the conversation, our relationship was in an entirely different place. We were back on track in a big way.

Over the course of the last ten years, I have had several different coaches. I have paid for some, others have coached me as part of a longer term business relationship. The organisation I have worked for has paid for others.

A few years ago, I had the privilege to work with an incredible woman called Elaine.

She rocked my world. From the moment I met her, I knew I wanted to spend as much time around her as possible, learning just how she crafted her sentences the way she did, wanting to discover whether I could absorb any of her wisdom and play it through in my own life.

Elaine changed my life. She took my thinking and my way of being to an entirely new level.

And then we literally lost her. Parts of this book are my small way of continuing her legacy and carrying on with the parts of her that I learned to adopt in my own life.

I got to work with her for two years and I am eternally grateful for every second of conversation I had with her.

Can you even imagine what it might feel to have someone like that in your life?

As a consequence of brilliant coaching, I have been able to break through so many issues that were affecting my inner peace. Even better, I have been able to create and design a life I am completely in love with - all because of skilful honest conversations.

Try it if you haven't already. Shop around carefully. Look for someone you really connect with and who you can sense right from the start really understands where you're coming from and then *show up*. Say what you would never say in public and watch just how quickly you start to unpick some of those knots inside you.

Coaching is not just for sticky moments either. I never cease to be amazed at how many people rock up to coaching sessions and say, '*I'm fine, I don't need coaching*' before we create sheer magic.

On many occasions I have used a coach to help me fire up my action to the next level or simply to help me grow and discover new things about myself.

I love to use my coach for 'rocket fuel' – an incredible concoction of momentum, inspiration, belief and energy - so that I can be out in the world serving other women even more powerfully.

Understanding *yourself* is key to your growth.

A great coach is going to help you unlock all kinds of talents and inner strength, they can stretch you and challenge you in ways that are beyond your imagination. If you take this path alone, the journey will be slower, more frustrating and you may never realise what you have within you.

Honestly – it's that important.

Go, find the one that lights you up – what are you waiting for?

REFLECTION

1. *Who in my life stretches me and offers me challenge?*

2. *How can I create more time with them that they would love as much as I do?*

3. *How would it feel to have someone in my life who believes in me without judgement and who will remind me of what I am truly capable of?*

CHAPTER 16

PLACES THAT GROUND US

'THERE IS NO WI-FI IN THE FOREST, BUT YOU WILL FIND A BETTER CONNECTION.'

UNKNOWN

Hands up if you love the idea of going on a retreat or one of those luxury holidays where you get to be quiet and looked after. If every now and then you just long for space and fresh air and someone else to cook the food. A world where you could just close your eyes, rest and get away from it all.

How's this for a thought:

Wouldn't it be amazing if we all built lives we didn't need to take a retreat from?

I can tell some of you are swearing right now. Thinking I'm off in some cuckoo land and internally shouting, *'does she even UNDERSTAND my life?'*.

No, I don't. Not one little bit.

I understand what we're up to as a collective though. And so do you. It's one of those things you're pretending not to know.

You. Have. Chosen. Your. Life.

You are continuing to make choices about it every single day. They're all caught up in those 'can'ts' and 'shoulds' and 'musts' again for sure. You are making the choices.

So let me say something else you already know.

You can choose to make different ones and you don't need to have bucket loads more money or time to create them. *Make something different out of what you already have.*

If you love the thought of what a retreat brings you, bring some of it into your life regularly.

It's so much simpler than you think.

Get out a piece of paper and write down all the places you love to be.

Sure, you can put a few foreign countries on there if you like, and you already know that you're not going there every day – they're up there with your retreat places.

Especially focus on the places that are within easy driving distance or even better, walking distance from where you live or work. The park around the corner from the office, the villages that are only ten minutes away from your home, the cycle path that winds its way through your town. Note down any place you can think of where there's water – canal paths, ponds, lakes. These places are all around you and by their very nature, they slow you down.

Now put them in your life.

Put them in your diary if you have one.

Schedule time to be in those places that ground you.

Let's be really clear here, I'm talking about the places that have that air of retreat about them.

When we used to live in a village out in the country, there was a 2 mile walk around the back of the village that no-one but me ever seemed to use. If I needed to get grounded, I'd stick the lead on Scruffy and off we'd go. Walking by fields and waving at the sheep (I actually do that).

No mobile phone in my pocket, just a couple of bags to pick up the poo (from the dog, obviously).

Walking and breathing. Walking and breathing. And noticing.

The grass, the wildflowers growing and changing, the rabbits when they appeared.

Now I live in the city again, I'm blessed with a view of the river and a beach just half an hour down the road.

I can walk along the water right outside my flat, or I can head to the beach and soak in the multiple breeds of dogs jumping up and down in the water and rolling in the sand. It's a place that makes me smile. It reminds me I have so much to be grateful for and very little to worry about.

You have these places within access of where you are right now.

Your soul needs them more than any shopping trip. Your creativity needs them more than any trip to the cinema. Your leader in you needs them to top up your energy bank and your drive.

They are more essential than you can ever imagine.

Schedule them in.

This way, you can access a moment of perspective and calm whenever you want.

Isn't it amazing what reveals itself when we make life easy?

REFLECTION

1. *Where are my places that ground me in the world?*

2. *Where are the ones I can get to within half an hour?*

3. *When am I going? (Sooner than that, go again)*

CHAPTER 17

THE MIND BODY CONNECTION

'AND I SAID TO MY BODY, SOFTLY, 'I WANT TO BE
YOUR FRIEND', IT TOOK A LONG BREATH AND REPLIED,
'I'VE BEEN WAITING MY WHOLE LIFE FOR THIS.'

NAYYIRAH WAHEED, 'THREE'

I consciously draw this book to a close by focussing on the body.

So many of us have this strange relationship with this huge gift we have been given.

I used to describe myself as a head being carried around by a body.

My body was this inconvenient thing that couldn't go as fast as I wanted it to, consume the crappy foods I wanted it to, exercise the way I wanted to. It held me back. What a dreadful way to look at the glorious unique vehicle I have been given to carry me through life.

I'm not interested in weight loss, or calorie burning or you honing your body to become an athlete.

I'm interested in you *recognising* that your body is full of *wisdom*.

I'm interested in you realising that having a positive relationship with your body and allowing it to become a guiding star when you seek counsel for what to do next is going to be a game changer for you.

I'm interested in you discovering embodiment.

What I mean here, wonderful, clever lady, is that *you have a* BODY *as well as a* MIND.

Not only do you have a body, you have almost certainly forgotten to notice that the human body, *your body*, is probably the most amazing bit of machinery that walks planet Earth.

Stay with me on this.

I'm speaking to the, conservatively speaking, 80% plus of you who really *DON'T LIKE YOUR BODY VERY MUCH AT ALL*. (You other 20%, I am just doing a little jump of excitement for you that this particular chapter is one you can pretty much sail through).

I'm speaking to those of you who adopt a fascinating strategy of extremes.

You have a process of hating your body and sending it daggers every time you happen to catch sight of it in a mirror, periodically filling it with junk food till it is full to bursting and topping that up with a selection of your favourite alcoholic drinks, before dragging it along to some kind of vigorous exercise regime that you pretty much detest, because you must *punish* it for not being able to handle all that rubbish food and drink without gaining a little extra comfort around the waistline.

Yes that sentence was deliberately long. I wanted you to feel how *tiring* it is. I wanted you to read it without taking a breath, wondering, *'when is this going to end?'.* See any parallels?

You top the icing on this particular cake with a good old dose of *'I don't need sleep or rest, I am Superwoman and can do everything'* and then, frankly, have the cheek to get frustrated when the body actually declares it is in fact quite tired and promptly catches a cold.

I wish I was being extreme.

If you've really got this pattern nailed, you also spend half of your time self-attacking for being 'bad' when it comes to food, getting really frustrated when others are not eating healthily in your household (as you are a master at pretending you are), stuffing chocolate bars in your face in the car on the way home and talking about food and weight constantly.

Really? What an excellent recipe for a joyful life.

Or, you know, *NOT*.

Let's talk about embodiment as an alternative then.

YOUR BODY KNOWS WHAT IT NEEDS

I like to think of embodiment as the practice of tuning into what the body actually needs, rather than looking to Google for the answers, or your friends, who also hate their bodies and berate themselves for being, 'bad'.

The core difference between looking to Google for answers and tuning into the body is that Google will have about a gazillion contradictory answers flying around to almost every single question you might have around weight loss, exercise and nutrition.

The body on the other hand, will give you crystal clear signals about what it needs and wants *all of the time.*

It is that clever.

Let's be honest, you've been tuning out those signals for a long, long time.

You've been believing it's far better to go with whatever new fad your friend has just picked up on;

far better to keep doing what you've always done even though it has failed you miserably up to this point;

far better to keep trying to hate your body into health.

I want to be clear on my stance here.

My desire for you is that you have a body that functions as well as it possibly can and that your mind is fed and nourished. I have no judgement whatsoever on what weight your body should be or how you look. I am interested in your brain having all the nourishment it needs to create great things in the world and your body functioning and maintaining health so that you can live a long and impactful life.

ENERGISING MOVEMENT

My advice to you is simple:

When it comes to exercise, the body needs to move to stay supple and strong. *You know this.*

Here's one simple question for you to think about,

'If all exercise delivered exactly the same calorie burn and therefore the only difference was how much I ENJOYED and LOVED TO PARTICIPATE in each type, what would I choose?'.

Got an answer?

Great.

Choose that. Do it regularly.

Then notice a few things.

Notice how much easier it is to put those shoes on when you actually *love* going out for a walk.

Notice how much you look forward to that yoga or pilates class when the body gets to stretch out and release all that tension.

Notice how much you smile when you finally learn to dance the way you always wanted to.

Once again, this is how you make it easy. Do *more* of what you *love*.

Connect with that body of yours - let it move around in the ways it loves the most.

A note of caution here: if you get injured every time you do Kick Boxing, take a good look at that. It's just a tiny bit possible the body is saying no to this one and you've got all hung up on calorie burn again. Part of listening to your body is noticing when it's telling you to stop. If Kick Boxing is not for you, let it go and try something that is. Take it from one who learned the hard way, the stop message is one you want to pay attention to.

LIGHT BULB
MOMENT

I'm a terrible runner. Truly. People can walk half marathons faster than I can run them. Brilliantly, I can speed walk a marathon faster than I can run one. FACT.

But I love to run. I especially like to test out how far I can run.

This has proven to be a particularly stupid idea on more occasions in my life than I can tell you. My body is perfectly happy to do a 5K run, maybe a 10K. Beyond that, it literally shuts down. My back starts to ache (this is more serious than it used to be since surgery), sometimes I get a stress fracture in my foot. I regularly experience fatigue on levels that are dramatically disproportionate to the exercise I have undertaken.

My body could not be clearer that distance running is not the exercise for me.

On the other hand, when I do pilates or swim, my body weeps with gratitude. My muscles elongate and the tension in my shoulders disappears.

A long-standing obsession with calories and my weight would have me ditch pilates and swimming for long distance running every single time.

For some reason, I love to think, *'this time it will be ok. I just need to train differently, build slower, eat better'.*

It doesn't matter what I do, my body will put the brakes on.

For a long time, what I failed to notice, was that my various injuries took me out for months at a time, negating every effort I had made to try to burn vast quantities of calories anyway.

I don't run anymore. My body thanks me for it daily.

Move your thoughts to one side on this one and let your body take control.

Let your body choose. Then move with it. It really does know best and it's time you started listening.

FOOD THAT NOURISHES US

You need nourishing food in order to have a healthy body and a healthy brain and to create the energy that you need to get on with living the life you want.

The other half of the embodiment equation is nourishing the body with great food, whilst *still* allowing the body to direct your decisions.

That means the Crazy Lady does not call the shots, your friends who obsess with food all day long do not call the shots, Google does not call the shots and nor does your local weight loss club.

Your body knows what it needs.

This is another thing you know you know by the way. It's just there is a high chance you have temporarily forgotten it. You don't need to read loads of stuff on what to eat. You don't need guidance from a million different websites. *You need to listen to your body and give it what it is asking for.*

Here are a few clues that you are NOT giving your body what it is asking for:

- You're hungry all the time (even you can work this one out). *More food please.*

- You're stuffed to the gills when you go to bed at night. *Less food at night please.*

- You have a bit of trouble going to the toilet. *More fibre and fresh veg please.*

- You're tired in the afternoon. More energy based food please. *Think Nuts not Mars Bars.*

- You have spots and greasy skin. *More essential fats please (think avocado, olive oil, oily fish, dairy). Oh, and less sugar.*

We can just make this super simple if you like. The less that comes out of a packet, the better. The more colourful your plate, the better (unless you're filling it with Skittles - good effort though). The less sugar, the better.

Commit to learning to interpret the signals. You haven't been doing it for a very long time, or if ever, so be patient. Most of us have no idea what our body needs because we've been overriding it for the best part of our lives. Listen intently.

Here's a revolutionary one to get you started.

When the body is tired, it is asking for SLEEP not coffee or a chocolate bar. If you really can't give it sleep (i.e. you're at work and the boss isn't keen on napping at your desk) then go for something natural, you know, nuts, fruit, veggies, maybe a spot of ginger if you can get it in a juice somewhere.

This is so very easy if you let it be.

(By the way, I know we're talking about food here and notice this too – if you're tired, you tend to make poor food choices. Before you know it, you're in a vicious cycle of re-energising through sugar or caffeine or alcohol or a cocktail of all three and you can't seem to find your way to making good choices again. Give your attention to rest first and you might be surprised about how your thoughts around food change.)

Your body will *NEVER* ask you for half a bottle of vodka, a giant bar of chocolate or a tub of ice cream. Never. It's not where it gets its best energy sources from.

And, sometimes, you're going to have those foods anyway, and frankly, SO YOU SHOULD! Because we all need permission to experience *pleasure*.

I was recently at an event with Nigella Lawson, the woman who has made generous, simple and indulgent home cooking a popular thing around the world. The interviewer asked her about her guilty pleasures when it came to food. She smiled, 'I don't associate those two words together. What does that even mean? Why would we have guilt when it comes to pleasure?'.

Round of applause that woman.

Pleasure is a most excellent thing in your life. *Just don't kid yourself that the body is asking you for it.* Once you have deeply enjoyed whatever it is you have chosen, reassure your body that you're not about to dive into a mountain of pizza and that you will continue to give it the love and nourishment it needs to thrive.

There are always going to be days we want to sit on the couch, watch TV and check out a little. All well and good – providing you don't let the Crazy Lady issue you with lectures all the way through. Because that somewhat defeats the point. Especially when it comes to the importance of pleasure.

Did you know your taste buds contain pleasure receptors? They're actually part of what tells the brain you are full.

So the other thing you need to do, as well as give your body food that nourishes it, is *slow down*. Enjoy the food. Savour it.

Take pleasure from it, in order to create the sensations your body needs to signal fullness and encourage you to stop eating.

Remember that 'retreat mentality'? Eating time is another time to bring it into play. Another little mini retreat every day of your life.

I truly believe the biggest change you can make around tuning into your body and giving it what it wants when it comes to food is this.

EAT SLOWLY and ENJOY WHAT YOU EAT.

If you tune into enjoyment, if you really take note of what you like and what you don't like, you'll get some amazing signals from your body. If you eat slowly, you can savour that food and really get the most from it (thus eliminating the panic some of us suffer that we'll never allow ourselves to have a certain thing again). What's more, your body can send signals to the brain that it has had enough thank you very much and your brain and you, can respond to those signals and stop eating.

That's it.

Never read a diet book again.

I mean it.

REFLECTION

1. *What are the messages from my body I am consistently ignoring?*

2. *What's the impact of me ignoring them?*

3. *What's the movement that my body really loves? When will I do it in the next 7 days?*

4. *What will I do in the next 24 hours to respect the things my body is requesting?*

5. *What does my body really need to keep it nourished right now?*

6. *Did I write that based on what I think it should need or what it's telling me it needs?*

7. *What would it take for me to give my body real attention over the next 7 days?*

8. *How can I make it easier to respond to what my body needs? What needs to go onto my shopping list and come off it?*

IT ALL COMES DOWN TO THIS

CHAPTER 18

BE YOU

'A WOMAN IN HARMONY WITH HER SPIRIT IS LIKE A RIVER FLOWING. SHE GOES WHERE SHE WILL WITHOUT PRETENCE AND ARRIVES AT HER DESTINATION PREPARED TO BE HERSELF AND ONLY HERSELF.'

MAYA ANGELOU

I've got so much more I want to share with you. I culled the last 20 pages of this book, even though I really loved them because I realised I was starting something new and you already have plenty here to make tiny easy changes that will shift your world.

And they are all easy. Truly. You make them hard by thinking about them and letting that voice in your head tell you that you don't have time or space or that you never finish anything you start.

It's just noise.

From today, decide to stop reminding yourself why you can't do things and get moving. If you need a friend to hold you accountable, find one. If you need more options, create them. If you need to uncover the science to check what I'm saying is accurate, off you go and check it out.

Get started.

When you are not getting what you want in life, ask yourself the question, *'how am I in my own way right now?'* and follow it up with, *'what would make this easy?'* and believe you can.

You have all you need to get going.

I still want to talk to you about speaking your truth powerfully, creating a new dimension in your relationships and the impact I am simply longing for you to have in the world.

That's all coming. For now, simply understand this, the final point:

Be You.

So many of us have built our lives on being what we think others want us to be. Heck, I built my career on it. I literally used to walk into a room and be like that bit in 'Pretty Woman' where Richard Gere asks Julia Roberts her name and she says, *'Whatever you want it to be'*.

My life got so much easier when I decided to be me. Unequivocally and proudly me. To honour my strengths and to be excited by my talents. To do more of what I loved and less of what I didn't. To be with the people who inspired me and not with those who sucked the life out of me. I consider these things as critical now. I will not compromise them for anything.

There is only one time *ever* in the world that you get to be the human being you are right now.

My desire for you is that you squeeze every drop of life out of it, that you live boldly and lovingly and generously - that we get to benefit from having the version of you that was designed to thrive in the world instead of the one who is trying to be what she thinks everyone else wants.

Dedicate your life to uncovering who you are and what you are here for.

Look your fears in the eye and smile. They are a sign that you are on the right track.

Stop listening to the voice in your head who says you can't.

YOU CAN.

Get out of your own way.

Be you. Proudly, brilliantly, uniquely.

That's who you were made to be.

WHAT DANIELLE MACLEOD IS UP TO:

Remarkable Women – Women the world is talking about

I form one half of Somebody Inside alongside the exceptional Nic Devlin.

As a pair, we run a number of events and programmes for women, including Women in Leadership corporate programmes for organisations who understand that now is the time to help women shape their own unique form of compelling and inspiring leadership.

We both believe that our power comes from mastering our mind. From recognising that thoughts are not always accurate or truthful and learning to dance with them in a way that reduces stress and anxiety and replaces it with joy and exuberance. We believe that the only person ever holding you back is you and we are excited by the opportunity that creates for you to have the life you long for.

My deep soul desire is to see more female leadership in the world. No angry feminist, I believe passionately that we need to find balance and space for the brilliance of *both* men and women for the sake of a balanced world. I teach heart-centred leadership and the limitless potential of all human beings to do more than they even imagine is possible. I believe that we have the capability to solve the world's problems, we simply need to believe we can.

In 2018, I opened the first Remarkable Women community, for women who want to explore the impact they could create in the world if only they would let themselves. It's a place for mind-blowing creations, bold thinking and to lean into other incredible women to discover just what we are capable of collectively and individually. We are already making the kind of magic the world is crying out for.

Women work with me for Rocket Fuel, Inspiration and Tiny Steps that create Huge Momentum. I work with them because without fail, they rock my world and make me proud to be on the same planet.

If you know you want to be a Remarkable Women (you already are by the way) and you want to make a bigger impact in the world whilst leading a life you love, or you are simply interested in learning more about my work, get in touch with me directly: danielle@somebodyinside.com.

I'd truly love to hear from you.

14037194R00098

Printed in Great Britain
by Amazon